IN THE SHADOW OF JOSEPH

Letters from Prison

By [Rev.] Thomas P. Bird, [41458]
Rev. Kenneth P. Kothe
and Dave Racer

Foreword by Governor Al Quie

LUTHERAN NEWS, INC.
684 Luther Lane
New Haven, MO 63068

In the Shadow of Joseph: Letters from Prison

ISBN 0-9702509-5-9

Copyright © 2004; Lutheran News, Inc., Thomas P. Bird, Rev. Kenneth P. Kothe, Dave Racer

All rights reserved. No reproduction in all or in part in any form is authorized without express written permission.

Mr. Racer has used the New King James Translation for his meditations; Nelson Bibles.

http://www.alethospress.com
http://www.cagedbird.net
http://www.tombird.net
http://www.daveracer.com

Printed by Morris Publishing
Kearney, Nebraska

Cover art by Danielle Dinger, St. Paul, Minnesota

10 9 8 7 6 5 4 3 2 1

Contents

Foreword: By Governor Albert Quie v

Section I 1
    Joseph's Case 3
    Tom Bird's Case 7

Section II: The Letters 19

    Forgive when forgotten 21
        Genesis 40:14&23

    The Rehab of Rahab 26
        Hebrews 11:31

    Full of Meanness or Meaningfulness 30
        Genesis 39:20-24

    Birdicus 36
        Proverbs 17:15

    Escapades of Escape 41
        I Corinthians 10:13

    Pomp & Circumstantial Evidence 46
        Genesis 44:14ff

    Brothers and Cisterns 51
        Genesis 37:21

    My Asenath 56
        Genesis 42:45

    Clothes Make the Man 61
        Genesis 37:33

    A Rock at Rock Bottom 66
        Genesis 49:24

    Father Figuring 70
        Genesis 37:34

    When Milestones Become Millstones 75
        Genesis 39:2

    On Wheat, Weeds & Waiting 81
        Genesis 37:19-20

On Setting the Record Straight Genesis 41:14	87
Unique But Not Special Genesis 37:2	92
And Life Goes On Genesis 38:1	98
There is a Bomb in Gilead Genesis 37:25	103
Shackles for Shekels Genesis 37:28	109
Letting Go of Your Benjamin Genesis 43:11	115
Yearn to Learn Psalm 105:17-22	121
Body Disposition Form Exodus 13:19	127
The Law of the Jungle Gen. 39:20-21	132
Half Full, Half Empty, A Drop Genesis 39:20-21	138
No Crying in Prison Genesis 43:30-31	144
Guilt Rides the Guilt-Ridden Genesis 42:21	150
Prison of Pity Genesis 42:36	156
Forgiving Living Genesis 50:15-21	162
About the Authors	170

Foreword

Trusting Christ Only

By Al Quie

This book reveals the thoughts and feelings of two ordained pastors of the Lutheran Church-Missouri Synod. The main character, Tom Bird, no longer bears the title of "Reverend" in that he is incarcerated, convicted of murder. Rev. Ken Kothe is Tom's long time friend and fellow seminarian. Dave Racer, the third writer, wrote *Caged Bird*, a book about Tom's life. Pastor Kothe and Mr. Racer believe Bird is innocent of the charges for which he has been convicted.

Tom Bird is but one of approximately two million people imprisoned in America. Each inmate's life also touches communities of millions of more people — family, friends, jail keepers, taxpayers. An unknown number of inmates are innocent — wrongfully convicted — but a judge or jury believed otherwise. Many inmates believe they have received an unjust sentence, especially when compared to others who have done similar crimes. I have met and talked with scores of these men.

What makes me sit up and take notice is when a person in prison with whom I have become close speaks of his crime saying, "I have no excuse, I did it because I was evil." Or another says, "Even though I don't like being here and want to get out as soon as possible, I'm glad I was sent to prison, because here Jesus Christ came into my life." It stirs my soul when a man in prison says, "I am free, free in Christ." Tom Bird, in this sense, is certainly a free man.

When a person claims to be innocent, however, I am filled with all sorts of mixed feelings. Is he telling the truth? If so, what went wrong with our criminal justice system? When I read about a person who has been found innocent after many years in prison, I am ashamed for the lost time the state kept him separated from his community.

Whether a person is guilty or innocent, though, we readers cannot once again adjudicate these cases; but we can be their friend. What each person in prison needs is a friend. Not a friend in place of Jesus Christ, but a friend through which the Spirit of God can work and who will minister to their unique needs.

Many people, and often for valid reasons, are fearful of being a friend to an incarcerated person. I felt this way for a substantial part of my life. However, one night, home late from work in Congress, I picked up my Bible for meditation before crawling into bed. The prior day, I had read Matthew 25:1-30. Now I planned to read to the end of the chapter, beginning with verse 31, where Jesus speaks about His second coming. As I read, at first I felt pretty good about myself because of what Jesus says about our actions on behalf of "the least of these," and that serving their needs is the same as serving Jesus. As a member of Congress and a Christian citizen, I had consciously put these practices into action. Then I read verse 36. "I was in prison and you came to visit me." Always before I had just let those words pass by. That night, I could not. After reading verses 44-46, I sat condemned and knew I had to do something about it.

That reading began a change in how I lived my life. It led to Bible studies in Lorton Penitentiary, the prison for Washington, D.C. It led to befriending Charles Colson and it grew into a deep love for incarcerated people, and a friendship with many of them. Friendship and fellowship in Christ brings about wonderful, fulfilling changes.

So as I reviewed *In the Shadow of Joseph*, it became fascinating to see how the thoughts of Tom Bird and his old friend Pastor Kothe unfolded during the years they exchanged these letters. I struggled with the earlier chapters; because at the same time I was reading Dave Racer's book *Caged Bird* that detailed Tom Bird's conviction and incarceration. I started with doubts about Tom

Bird's innocence and felt anger at what seemed to me to be his indiscriminating naiveté; I felt impatience with Ken Kothe who I thought was trying too hard to make Tom appear as he wanted him to be. But, by the end of *Caged Bird*, I said that Tom must be innocent of the charges; he had let himself become entrapped by some poor decisions that led jurors to see him as guilty.

So I read *In the Shadow of Joseph* with a sense of who Tom is and how he got into his predicament. I read his letters with special interest, to see how he deals with his predicament. Then I read Pastor Kothe's responses to Tom's letters; they gave themselves to a great deal of teaching in the earlier letters. I saw how in later letters he began to give way to personal revelations about his own struggles — because we all have struggles. Dave's meditations nicely tie together each pair of letters, giving them a broader application for those imprisoned and us on the outside.

I found Chapter 20 of particular interest as Tom wrote about the question of trust. Although Ken and Dave seem to agree with Tom, they have a bit of trouble with the idea that a man cannot trust other men. For me, Tom had caught the meaning of the Gospel at John 2:24, how Jesus did not entrust Himself to any man. John further wrote in I John the words that are often repeated in our liturgy: "If we say we have no sin, the truth is not in us." But, how can a person live their life if they do not trust anyone? Jesus wants our total trust in Him in the same way that a small child trusts a parent. And the truth is that, eventually, every child finds some chink in the presumed perfection of their parent.

Two other chapters especially stood out for me. They deal with the subjects of being careful not to be trapped, and weeping. We can look back at events in our lives and see the results of our choices, but when we realize the grace and mercy of our Lord and Savior Jesus Christ, there is a great release from our mistakes. And I am moved by Tom's words in Letter 24, "No Crying in Prison." Tears are the language of the angels. Men love to fix things and especially resist their natural emotions; but there are many things that only God can fix and Tom shows us this in a most dramatic way.

By working with prisoners, I have become more dependent on

God. Tom's writing, the responses they generated from Pastor Kothe and Dave Racer further show that God is totally sufficient for all our needs.

Al Quie served as Minnesota's Governor from 1979-1983. Prior to that, he served in the United States Congress as a Representative from Minnesota's First Congressional District. In 1954, he had won a Minnesota State Senate seat at the same time he operated the family farm.

Gov. Quie and his wife Gretchen were married in 1948. They have five children and numerous grandchildren.

Gov. Quie has served on many boards including Prison Fellowship Ministries, Lutheran Brotherhood Mutual Funds, Lutheran Health Systems, Tentmakers, Vesper Society, Nobel Peace Prize Forum, Search Institute, Council on Crime and Justice, Urban Ventures, AGORA, the Commission on Excellence in Education that wrote "A Nation at Risk," and Word Alone. Several of these are currently on his agenda. He also is a sought-after speaker, and serves as mentor to many individuals.

Gov. Quie is a member of Minnetonka Lutheran Church, Minnesota, and is a voting member of the Evangelical Lutheran Church in America Church-Wide Assemblies.

Gov. Quie's own book, Riding the Divide, *was released in 2003, documenting his horseback ride across the Continental Divide from the Canadian to New Mexico border. See the book at* http://www.ridingthedivide.com

Neckties are considered "escape paraphernalia" and inmates do not wear suits in prison. Tom Bird managed to have this photograph taken several months before the release of *Caged Bird* (2000).

This photograph of Tom Bird was taken during his days as Senior Pastor at Faith Lutheran Church, Emporia, Kansas (1983)

Caged Bird

Dave Racer's book that chronicles Tom Bird's convictions and attempts to win justice.

Reverend Kenneth P. Kothe,
Pastor of Redeemer Lutheran
Church, Burnsville, MN

Dave Racer
Author, speaker, writer;
President of
Alethos Press LLC
St. Paul, MN

Dedication

With gratefulness to God for His faithfulness.

To the men and women behind bars who make their walk with Jesus Christ their first priority; to those who have been rightfully convicted of crimes, but want to be set free for eternity; to those who have been wrongfully convicted, and seek hope; to all the families of inmates; to those living outside prisons made with bricks, bars and mortar, but live incarcerated by sin and faithlessness.

To Rev. Ralph E. Bird, who wrote a letter each day for 17 years to his son Tom, his writing interrupted only by Christ's calling him to Himself.

Acknowledgements

This book had matured over the course of many years. It is the result of all of us trying to find what good can come from Tom Bird's predicament. To publish it required the help of dozens and even hundreds of faithful people; some supported Tom Bird and our work in prayer; some contributed to his legal fund and to help defray the costs of this book; others cared for our families and continued the fight for justice.

At the risk of leaving out many who ought to be specifically mentioned, the authors especially want to extend thanks to:

Rev. Earl Bielefeld and Rev. David Spaeth for the articles and letters they wrote, and the funds they raised to help Tom Bird.

Rev. Herman Otten for keeping the story alive by his frequent publication of stories about Tom Bird in *Christian News*. Without Pastor Otten and his newspaper, this book would not have been published.

Terry Bird, Katherine Kothe and Rosanne Racer, our wives, whose patience and prayers make it possible for us to continue our work.

Gov. Al Quie and the hundreds of like-minded persons who regularly seek out and minister to incarcerated persons.

Section I:

Joseph's Case

Tom Bird's Case

Tom Bird: Modern Day Joseph?

Pastor Kothe's Commitment

Letters from Prison

Joseph's Case

The headline read:

> **Joseph arrested in sex scandal**
> **Potiphar's wife charges assault**

Soon the headline changed:

> **Joseph sentenced to life in prison**
> **High official falls from favor**

Joseph's roller-coaster life is chronicled in Genesis 30-50. It is a human story of absolute sorrow and abandonment. It is a spiritual story of absolute victory and abiding faith. It is a story of the failure of civil law, violation of God's Law and the fidelity of God's grace.

Try to imagine Joseph's state of mind and emotions after his arrest. Potiphar's wife tried for many days to seduce him, but he refused. One day she grabbed for him aggressively enough to pull off his cloak. Then she claimed that he had tried to rape her and held up his cloak as proof. She had weak circumstantial evidence - her own witness and Joseph's cloak - but enough to convict Joseph. In that criminal system, his crime meant life in prison with no hope of release.

Prior to his arrest, Joseph had served in a position of high calling where his master and staff depended on his integrity, honesty and moral character. In charge of all of Potiphar's affairs, Joseph would also have gained great respect in his community. No doubt, Joseph had also learned and practiced the need to keep quiet about indiscretions of those in Potiphar's household. For this, he had been awarded the complete trust of the master, a trust he did not abuse.

But Potiphar's wife, a temptress, seemed bent on becoming his lover. When rebuffed by Joseph, she wove a chilling tale of his debauched behavior toward her and charged him with a felony crime against which his only defense was his character.

He stood before the master and heard the charges against him. No record exists of whether Potiphar even allowed Joseph to tell his side of the story; to present a defense. Potiphar, bound by both the demands of his position and Egyptian law, needed to accept that his wife's charges against Joseph were true. The law instructed him that an Egyptian could not take the word of a slave over that of another Egyptian, and to do so would have brought shame on Potiphar's wife and disgrace on his household. So Potiphar sent Joseph, innocent and wrongfully convicted, to prison. Perhaps he saw lifetime imprisonment as a gesture of grace when he could have ordered the death penalty.

Wrongfully convicted and locked up in prison, Joseph talked with other inmates about his dilemma. Two of them had worked for Pharaoh, and when the cupbearer was later released to go back to Pharaoh, Joseph asked him to plead his case to Egypt's most powerful ruler. Since there was no appeals court in which Joseph could present his case, all he could do was hope that the cupbearer would keep his promise, and then continue in his prayers for release. At some point, it is likely Joseph resigned himself to a lifetime of incarceration.

The charges against Joseph were lies. The personal degradation Joseph suffered was, as borne by a man of such high moral character, excruciating.

This wrongful conviction stripped Joseph of his position and responsibility. Joseph sat in brutal surroundings. Worse, incarceration robbed him of his intense desire to live responsibly and above reproach in his community and sphere of influence. It stripped him of a productive outlet of his desire to serve by using his God-given talents and abilities for the betterment of others. And he had done nothing illegal.

Some may suggest that Joseph committed an error in judgment by going to Potiphar's wife, especially once he knew of her evil intent. Yet, as the master of Potiphar's household, he had a duty to respond to her. Had he not gone to her, she could never have seized his cloak. His sense of duty and responsibility placed him in a vulnerable position. To serve Potiphar he had also to serve the master's philandering wife.

Stripped of the comforts offered by his former position and degraded in the community, Joseph sat in prison able only to grasp one reality; one reality that has no bars and cannot be incarcerated. It is the one reality that sets men and women free. God. Joseph knew God. Joseph worshiped God. God's Spirit enabled him to grasp the reality that God walked with him.

While in prison, Joseph refused to give into his predicament and sought to become useful to the warden. As a result, he became an administrator in the prison bringing benefits to guards, inmates and, indirectly, the government that had wrongfully incarcerated him. To the outside world, and especially to Pharaoh's inner sanctum, Joseph no longer existed.

Then Pharaoh had a dream that greatly disturbed him. So convinced was he that this dream had a hidden message, he demanded that someone interpret it for him. No one in his inner sanctum could do so, but his cupbearer who had served prison time with Joseph had a suggestion. He remembered that Joseph had a gift of being able to interpret dreams. He had witnessed Joseph's willingness and ability to provide help. Pharaoh called Joseph out of prison.

After more than a decade of wrongful incarceration, Joseph left prison. Pharaoh's servants prepared Joseph to meet the king whereupon he listened patiently to the disturbing dreams. God gave him the interpretation, and he answered Pharaoh's distress. As a result, Pharaoh made Joseph his chief aide, his Prime Minister, and left many of the affairs of state in the hands of this ex-inmate.

Joseph reestablished his credibility as a trusted administrator and rose to the highest level of government. Yet, no record exists that in this lifetime he ever lost the label of a convicted fellow, guilty of attempted rape. God alone knew the truth of Joseph's innocence and He had removed that stigma from his eternal record.

Joseph's story has provided grist for thousands of sermons. Joseph's character has been examined under the microscope of exegesis, word and cultural studies. And no doubt, teachers and preachers have found in Joseph's life applications for just about all of us.

But how many people have had the unique experience of examining Joseph from the viewpoint of his own circumstances; from inside a prison while serving a life sentence as a result of a wrongful conviction? It is unlikely that such a story had yet to be written, until this book.

Tom Bird's Case

Parallels with Joseph

In 1972, 100 men gathered at Springfield, Illinois to begin attending Concordia Seminary together. Two of them, Thomas P. Bird from Arkansas, and Kenneth P. Kothe from Minnesota, found their commonality in the classroom and on the athletic fields. Little did they know that 12 years later, the State of Kansas would imprison one of them. Nor did they know that their lives would become entangled in a fight for freedom.

Following graduation from seminary in 1976, Ken and his wife Katherine took their family to Parker's Prairie in Northern Minnesota to begin their ministry. Tom and his wife Sandy went to West Memphis, Arkansas, where Tom served two churches. And the Birds became parents of three children.

Eventually, the Redeemer Lutheran Church in Burnsville, Minnesota, called Ken to become its Senior Pastor. Other than exchanging Christmas letters, mostly written by their wives, Ken heard little about Tom Bird. Ken had his own struggles within the church, both locally and nationally.

Ken fought charges brought by lay ministers who did not like his orthodox teachings on politically sensitive issues. Also, he had accused them of administrative mistakes that were hurting his congregation. They wanted Ken fired. During 1985, and again in 1987, Ken endured two heresy trials from which he was exonerated, but not without paying a terrible emotional, mental and financial price, including the loss of his home. A year later, a synod organization foreclosed on the church building; the local congregation could not meet its mortgage payments. The congregation rallied and, in June 1995, five hours before foreclosure would have become final,

Redeemer Lutheran swapped its church property with Good Shepherd Lutheran, a congregation a mile down the road.

So as Ken saw the turmoil developing in the life of his friend Tom Bird, he had an informed empathy for his brother. With the series of tragic events that began in 1983, Ken wrote to Tom to encourage him, and in 1984, wrote to Judge Gary Rulon, pleading for mercy for Tom. Then, spurred on by the release of the movie, Murder Ordained in 1987, Ken's life became entangled with Tom's in a way that resulted in the writing of the book, Caged Bird, in 2000. Caged Bird detailed Tom Bird's own Joseph story, at least as it concerns his wrongful conviction and lifetime incarceration.

Tragedy set to happen

Messiah Lutheran Church in Emporia, Kansas called Tom to be an Associate Pastor in 1982, but specifically for the purpose of leading the expansion of a new mission church-Faith Lutheran Church in Emporia. Attendance at Faith doubled twice in 18 months, imposing ever-greater responsibilities on Tom. Sandy took a part-time teaching position at Emporia State University and began working on her second Master's Degree. Life became tense and exhausting for both of them.

Faith Lutheran saw the need to provide administrative support for Tom and hired Lorna Anderson as their first paid church secretary. No one at the church knew, or was willing to admit, that Lorna had a well-earned reputation as a promiscuous woman. Nor did anyone know of the abortion of her first child that had been demanded by her college sweetheart or about the resultant psychological and spiritual damage it brought to her.

Soon after Lorna's hiring, Sandy Bird and some other churchwomen began to fear that Lorna had set her sights on Tom. Sandy became concerned enough to share it with Tom and with a few of her closest friends and family members.

Tom saw Lorna as a hurting woman in need of the tender healing touch of the Savior. He saw himself as the instrument through which God ministered to her.

Without his knowledge or involvement, Lorna began telling others that she and Tom were in love and that he was good in bed. At the same time, Lorna became very disturbed about her marriage to Martin Anderson and began talking with a few intimates about finding someone to murder him.

On July 17, 1983 a canoeist found Sandy Bird's body lying face down in the Cottonwood River just in front of her overturned car. It appeared that Sandy's car had gone over the riverbank next to an old steel, single lane bridge called "The Rocky Ford Bridge."

Sandy's death devastated Tom and his three young children. Police treated her death as a mysterious accident.

On July 26, Lorna Anderson told two close acquaintances that Sandy's death was no accident, but never explained to them why she thought this to be true. The women had no reason to pursue this with her and so, said nothing about it until questioned years later by prosecutors.

Lorna's actions and words following Sandy's death made it clear that she still considered Tom Bird, now a widower, to be her lover.

Then on November 4, 1983, 16 weeks after Sandy's death, in a ditch alongside a road just outside of Junction City, Kansas, someone murdered Martin Anderson by shooting three .22 caliber bullets into his head. Lorna stood nearby and her four young girls sat in a van just 50 feet away. They heard their daddy yell and they saw "sparkles."

Within days of Marty's murder, investigators learned of the alleged romantic link between Tom and Lorna. They reopened an investigation into Sandy's death.

Eight months later, a Lyon County jury found Tom Bird guilty of Solicitation to Commit the murder of Martin Anderson. Sensationalism about the allegations of sex and murder created a furor in Emporia and Junction City, Kansas, a furor that spread through national and even international media.

As Tom approached his trial he believed that in a court of law, truth prevailed. He also realized that though he claimed innocence, in Emporia his career had been ruined, integrity destroyed and character assaulted beyond repair. He believed that once the trial was over, he would be free to move elsewhere and start life anew. His strategy was simple; present a truthful defense and trust the court to apply the rules evenly. He took this for granted. He lost.

At Tom's trial, a judge allowed testimony that he admitted to be hearsay, and that testimony caught the jury's ear. Along with the testimony of Darrel Carter, an Emporia building contractor, Tom's fate was sealed. The jury believed Mr. Carter, a lifetime Emporia resident, rather than Pastor Bird.

Kansas' correctional professionals who examined Tom recommended immediate parole with no incarceration. Instead, Emporia Judge Gary Rulon enforced on him a sentence of 2-1/2 to 7 years in prison, and refused to grant bail even during his appeal. Kansas moved Tom to Lansing Correctional Facility in Lansing, Kansas early in September 1984.

Pressure began to build in Lyon County officials to prosecute Tom for the death of his wife. Early in 1985, Lyon County convened only the second grand jury in its history and from this came an indictment of Tom for the First-Degree murder of Sandra Stringer Bird.

The grand jury could not determine the manner in which Tom had allegedly killed his wife and wrote a vague indictment. The lack of clarity in the indictment placed Tom in the position of having to defend himself against unknown theories about how Sandy died. The effect of the vague indictment was to force Tom to convince a jury that other logical explanations existed for her death. He had to prove his innocence. Emporians saw an apparent violation of the kind of trust placed in a pastor, and held it against him.

The county attorney used the same hearsay evidence and Mr. Carter's testimony as in the first trial to prove motive. He presented a large volume of highly technical, incomprehensible and contradictory information as his evidence to prove the method by which Sandy died. And he presented no evidence that Tom came near the location of Sandy's death. Yet a Lyon County jury convicted Tom of murder. Trial records show that his conviction was accomplished despite being unable even to prove how Sandy died.

During both trials, the person who could have countered many of the state's arguments about motive kept quiet. Lorna Anderson pled protection against self-incrimination and, therefore, was not available to be cross-examined. This allowed prosecution witnesses to state as fact certain statements she had made to them, and left Tom with no adequate method to prove that they had not been lovers, providing a motive for the alleged crimes.

In early August 1985, Judge Gary Rulon sentenced Tom to life in prison for the murder of Sandy Bird. A series of appeals began, but those appeals fell on deaf ears, or on ears that were distracted by the sheer scandal of a pastor and his church secretary murdering their spouses.

It got worse

Once Tom had been convicted, the state convinced Lorna Anderson to tell them who really killed her husband Martin. They had already agreed to reduce Lorna's charges to two counts of Solicitation to Commit Murder, despite clear evidence that she had paid Danny Carter to hire a killer. A judge sentenced her to 5-18 years in prison. She hoped for a quick parole.

In a lengthy sworn statement, Lorna told investigators that Tom Bird murdered Martin Anderson. She described in graphic detail how Tom had committed the murder, and she told them where to find the gun. She also claimed that Tom had confessed to murdering his wife and this, likewise, she did with graphic detail-as though she might have been there.

With Tom locked away in prison, investigators worked hard to fill the gaping holes in Lorna's statement. Especially gnawing was Tom's solid alibi, the testimony of a young girl and four others who saw him an hour away in Topeka at the time of Marty's murder.

Meanwhile, CBS and 23 other producers responded to a story about Tom Bird and Lorna Anderson that ran in the March 1986 edition of *The Los Angeles Times*. CBS beat the others to the punch and on May 3 and May 5 of 1987, aired *Murder Ordained*. CBS claimed it was the Tom Bird story, based on the true story of his life. The main characters in the movie, Tom and Sandy Bird, Marty and Lorna Anderson, and their children, had no input into the movie (none of the Bird family members were interviewed), yet it depicted intimate scenes that supposedly took place among them all.

Murder Ordained devastated Tom and his family, and it destroyed any chance he had to win his appeals, though he never quit trying.

Finally, frustrated by the lack of progress in their investigation, the Geary County Attorney charged Lorna with the First-Degree murder of Martin Anderson. She quickly negotiated a plea agreement to Second-Degree murder and agreed to testify against Tom Bird at trial. A Geary County judge sentenced Lorna to 15 years to life for the Second-Degree murder of Marty Anderson. For a time the state incarcerated her in a co-educational prison at Lansing Correctional Facility. Later they moved her to the Topeka Correctional Facility where she still resided in 2004, hoping to eventually win parole.

In March of 1990, Judge Melvin Gradert wrote these words in response to a motion brought by Mike McCone, Tom's attorney:
"The present crimes [the murder of Marty Anderson] and the prior crimes are but equal parts in a scheme. The crimes are so closely connected that their probative value overwhelms their prejudicial effect. This crime did not occur in a vacuum and proof of its commission and the identity of the actor should not be tried in a vacuum."

Judge Gradert's comments suggested the fact that Marty Anderson had been murdered, about which there could be no dispute, and the death of Sandra Bird, about which there was much dispute, were the same criminal scheme carried out by the same players. The players in this real life drama were the same; the motive was the same. Only the method and opportunity were different. Tom Bird agreed with Gradert's assertion, but he disagreed on his role in both crimes. He insisted on his innocence.

A Geary County trial jury found Tom Bird innocent of Marty Anderson's murder.

Why?

At the 1990 trial, Lorna Anderson took the witness stand for the first time in any of Tom's trials and admitted to more than 80 lies she had made in previous sworn statements. So many lies were proven that other prosecution witnesses, likewise, became unbelievable. And testimony provided by a young woman who had no motive to lie, showed that Tom could not possibly have been in Junction City during the murder. She and four others saw him in Topeka.

As Tom's family and friends wept tears of joy, sheriffs escorted Tom back to Lansing Correctional Facility to continue serving his life sentence for the murder of Sandy Bird. News stories across the state claimed it would be only a matter of time before Kansas released Tom, given the outcome of the 1990 trial.

Ten years later, as Caged Bird hit the bookstores, Tom Bird faced the Kansas Parole Board-still incarcerated for the wrongful murder conviction by that 1985 jury.

Early in October 2000, Tom gave the Kansas Parole Board an insight into the severe nature of his punishment. His words are paraphrased here:

> "Punishment is a relative thing. Many incarcerated men awake every morning, do nothing more than police cigarette butts in the Pod area, and then sit in their rooms all day. They play poker or pinochle late into the night. They have little or no contact with their children, families or spouses. They take no responsibility for anything outside the walls. Punishment for them is losing their freedom.
>
> "One day my wife [Tom married Terry in a 1988 ceremony at Lansing Correctional Facility] came to see me as she does twice every weekend. After she left, I watched her climb into her car. She had a flat tire.
>
> "I stood 100 yards from her, separated by chain link fence and razor wire, unable to even

help her change her tire. This is punishment. I can do absolutely nothing to help my family or to take responsibility for them."

The parole board expressed its delight with the way Tom's case for parole had been presented. Not only did he have scores of letters of support, the support of his three adult children, a job awaiting him, high psychological marks and a flawless prison record, he had remained actively engaged in a number of ministry efforts during his incarceration.

In 1986, Tom helped start a chapter of Convicts for Christ, ministering to the personal needs of his fellow inmates. Unlike most prison ministries, this organization was organized by an inmate for the betterment of other inmates.

He participated in the production of the video "Prison is a Place," as well as wrote, directed and edited another video, "The Heart of Prison."

Concordia Publishing House published his *Prisoner's Reflections: Meditations for Prisoners*.

In the late 1980s, he and his wife Terry started Marriage Enrichment seminars inside the prison walls for the express purpose of helping families remain intact. These annual seminars have brought strength and stability to families that otherwise would be devastated by the loss of their dad to imprisonment.

He and another inmate, Michael Bornholdt, held the Guinness World Record for a tennis marathon, played inside the prison during 1988. The two men played 125 hours and 10 minutes of continuous tennis before laying down their rackets. They raised more than $1,000 for the Ronald McDonald House from prisoners and others inside the walls. (The record was broken soon after their accomplishment, but by people on the outside of prison.)

Terry served on the board of "Outside Connections," a service ministry for adults who are visiting in prison. Housed in a small building directly across the street from Lansing Correctional Facility's front door, visitors can leave their children with attendants while they visit inside the prison.

Tom began working for Impact Design, a private business that employs inmates behind the prison walls. His supervisor claimed Tom was one of their three best employees and said, "He would do much more good on the outside than the inside." Tom worked as a Customer Service Representative, communicating by phone with scores of customers across the country, including some who worked in New York's World Trade Center. Late in 2001, Impact Design named Tom as a purchasing agent.

As the parole board began its dialog with Tom that October day, they made it plain that Kansas customarily does not parole prisoners with life sentences in less than 20 years. He had served but 15 years of the life sentence, and another year on the first charge.

Tom's parole attorney pled for leniency reminding the parole board of the most important of the mitigating factors surrounding his case-his innocence.

In February of 2001, Tom learned that the parole board had turned down his parole. They set his next eligibility for 2005-20 years after his conviction for murder.

Tom Bird, A modern day Joseph?

People will disagree, some rather angrily, about Tom's guilt or innocence. He has never wavered on this, though by doing so he might have won favor with the parole board. They seldom parole inmates who refuse to take responsibility for their crime.
Pastor Ken Kothe saw in Tom's life several parallels to Joseph's incarceration. They are hard to ignore.

>Both held positions requiring high moral character, trust and integrity.
>
>Both were entangled in a sex scandal.
>
>Both were found guilty though maintaining their innocence.
>
>Both were stripped of their dignity, integrity and character.

> Both were abandoned by the institutions that they had served.
>
> Both hung tightly to their faith in God in the face of extreme pressure.
>
> Both found ways to serve God despite their personal discomfort and distress.
>
> Both continued to cry out for relief.

Drawing a direct comparison between historic Biblical characters such as Joseph and modern men like Tom Bird carries great risk of judgment. Christians are quick to forgive the indiscretions of King David and Solomon, and have their faith built by the Bible's testimony of Joseph's fidelity. But no two persons ever experience the same events, and keen observers of Tom and Joseph will be sure to point out one glaring difference between the two men.

We are certain by the testimony of scripture, that Joseph resisted Potiphar's wife's seductions. The fact that no other record exists about this or any other similar incident most likely means that Joseph remained sexually pure all during his life.

There is, however, a record created by Tom Bird himself through a very painful confession that he did in fact, eventually, succumb to the temptress, Lorna Anderson, long after both their spouses had died. Tom confessed this in Caged Bird which contains his verbatim statement about the incident.

Years after that incident, Tom wrote to Pastor Kothe with these words: "For a Christian who has repented and has received the full forgiveness in Christ, bringing up past sins as a blame for present bad happenings actually results in cheapening the precious blood of Jesus Christ. Worse yet, for a Christian to succumb to the temptation to blame others such as 'the system' or 'the administration' gives a false sense of relief from personal guilt. Why do the guilt ridden let guilt ride our backs?"

"I have no way of knowing when Tom confessed his sin of fornication to God," Pastor Ken responded. "I just know this. In 1987, Tom made a confession of his sin to me. He accepted it for what it was, and repented of it. And he confessed the truth - that God, through Jesus Christ, fully forgave him of that sin."

Commitment blossomed

In 1999, Pastor Kothe made two significant commitments to his friend Tom Bird. One was to have a book written that would tell Tom's story from his point of view. It resulted in the book *Caged Bird* (Dave Racer, 2000, Alethos Press LLC, PO Box 600160, St. Paul, MN, 55106). The other was to begin an exchange of letters with Tom. Pastor Kothe originally called them, "Letters from a Modern Day Joseph."

Pastor Kothe asked Tom to bare his heart about prison life from the vantage point of a wrongfully convicted, innocent man. He asked him to examine his prison life in the context of Joseph's and to write openly and insightfully. By so doing, Pastor Kothe believed that Tom would produce letters filled with human drama that demonstrated how a life dedicated to God's service could be lived out under some of the harshest conditions known to man-lifetime imprisonment.

Pastor Kothe believed that Tom's love of God and passion for the Gospel would flow from the words on paper. He knew of Tom's abiding love for his children, wife and family. He believed as Tom put pen to paper, that the Holy Spirit would prompt Tom to lay himself open and vulnerable.

As Tom began to write, Pastor Kothe personally felt the impact of his words. He read of justice, love, mercy, truth and forgiveness. He knew that the letters would be therapeutic for Tom, but had not realized how deeply they would touch his own heart.

As Pastor Kothe responded to Tom's letters, a dialogue began that resembled that of a loving pastor and a parishioner, but as often as not, it was Tom's letters comforting Pastor Kothe rather than the other way around. And Pastor Kothe saw that the dialogue of letters would bring a challenge and comfort to those in his own church, so he decided to publish them in the church newsletter at Redeemer Lutheran Church, and in a weekly newspaper, "Christian News." For each letter Tom wrote, Pastor Kothe wrote an answer.

Taken together, the dialogue between Pastor Kothe and Tom Bird form a moving insight into the heart of two men in love with the God who can sustain hope, love and character under any circumstance. They demonstrate how the Holy Spirit breaks down all barriers, and how no walls, whether made of stone and steel, or of a deceit-filled sinful heart, can stand against the power of the Word of God.

The reader of these letters will reflect on their own life and find in them strength and motivation to face their own hardship. They will find God calling to them to let His Holy Spirit sustain them during their darkest days, and lift them into the light of His Love.

Tom makes no claim to be a spiritual giant like Joseph. Ken makes no claim to provide spiritual insight like Martin Luther. But their letters show two humans striving to live as God would have them live, no matter whom they are or what they face.

Perhaps Henry Blackaby best summed up what is going on in the exchange between these two men in his book, *Experiencing God*. He wrote, "What you do reveals what you believe about God regardless of what you say."[1]

---

[1] Henry Blackaby, *Experiencing God.* Nashville, Life Way Press; Page 119.

Section II:

The Letters

&

Meditations

Letter One:
Forgive Even When Forgotten

Genesis 40:14, 23

"Only keep me in mind when it goes well with you, and please do me a kindness by mentioning me to Pharaoh, and get me out of this prison...Yet the chief cupbearer did not remember Joseph, but forgot him."

Ken,

You and others have compared my situation with that of Joseph's of the Old Testament. I too am prone to look to Joseph-sometimes as a contrast, sometimes as a comparison. Joseph's life was more difficult than mine and I often fall short of his strength of character.

I admire Joseph as a phenomenal man of faith to be imitated whether out of prison or in prison. I seek the kind of determined, enduring faith that Joseph displayed as we look at the highs and lows of his lifetime.

Born the eleventh son; rose to prominence in his family; thrown into a pit out of jealousy, sold into slavery. Then in that slavery was escalated to a high position only to be falsely accused and thrust into prison. Even in prison Joseph was such a positive force that he was elevated to trustee.

In all this, Joseph maintained his persistent faith and an unfailing determination that the Lord would use him for a divine purpose. Joseph's life was far from painless. I can identify closely with Joseph in the episodes described in Genesis 40:14, 23.

Joseph had taken care of the Chief Cupbearer while he was in prison. When the Cupbearer left the prison Joseph had this one request: "...when all goes well with you, remember me and show me kindness, mention me to Pharaoh and get me out of this prison." Joseph knew that this Chief Cupbearer could very well be the key to his release. It was a sad day for Joseph when he realized the Chief Cupbearer had forgotten him. Hope in the Cupbearer had made prison life bearable for Joseph.

You ask me what would be my greatest fear in prison? Well, Ken, there are some rare dangers from violent men here. There is some concern with predators. I'm leery of unstable young gang members with seemingly nothing to live for and therefore, nothing to lose. Yet the Lord protects me. My greatest fear then is, like Joseph, that of being forgotten.

I am very blessed that I have a loving wife, children, family and, of course, friends like you. Yet there are some who have told me straight to my face that the only way I'll get out of here is laid out with a tag on my toe. Now I do not believe that I will die in here. Like Joseph, I believe the Lord will work this for the good of many (and really, the Lord already has; but that is another letter).

After two years, the Cupbearer remembered Joseph. Joseph was released-his family reconciled and restored. I am encouraged that the Lord has not forgotten me. I await the day of release holding on to the promise of Christ to restore me whether it be heavenward or homeward.

In His Peace,

Tom Bird

◆ ◆ ◆

Tom,

Your letter came today. It reminded me of some things I have done in my life that I want to forget but can't. Your fear of being forgotten opened up for me my fear of remembering, although there is both good and bad to remember.

Like Joseph, I, too, am born the eleventh son. My father, grandfather and great-grandfather all were pastors in the Lutheran Church Missouri Synod. In 1868, Dittmar Kothe came over from Germany to do mission work among the German community in Litchfield, Illinois. Since then, the Gospel has been passed on from generation to generation to me, and now to my family. This is a good memory for me, and a serious trust.

Then I read Genesis 40:14 and 23 again and thought the words prophetic and timely. The Cupbearer forgot Joseph. The Cupbearer got caught up in his own world, and quit thinking about Joseph.

I, too, have forgotten many important things: the needs of my wife and children, Redeemer's congregation, consideration and respect toward fellow pastors. Your letter especially reminds how I forgot you - a fellow-seminarian suffering and convicted for life.

It took me too long to recognize your suffering. I excused myself by saying I was too busy thinking about number one. For at the very moment when you needed a friend I was ensnared by my own problems. While you were on trial for your life, I was on trial for my teaching.

A member of my congregation had charged me with heresy as a result of my being tactless and unloving, a violation of Jesus' command, "...love one another even as I have loved you." I offended this man by constantly rebutting his every opinion if it disagreed with my own. I did this in Bible class on Sunday morning. My actions irritated him and his irritated me.

As a pastor, I knew that I should have simply restated the Biblical point, listened to his viewpoint, shut up and then moved on to the next verse. Instead, I continued the argument. My actions resulted in a church trial that drained me emotionally, physically and spiritually. And it negatively affected my ability to be a shepherd to my people.

I learned that allowing this verbal sparing to continue was both my fault and symptomatic of sin. I had forgotten true humility and how to speak the truth in love.

The results of my actions meant being distracted from another duty - ministering to you, a dear friend in need. I forgot you, my friend. I even forgot to pray for you.

Unlike me, though, Jesus never forgets His own. I know that brought me comfort during my trial, and likewise, brings you comfort during lonely days at Lansing.

Joseph spent some 13 years in prison as a forgotten man, and you have already surpassed that and likewise, have been equally forgotten. The only way most people remember you is when that awful movie, *Murder Ordained*, is shown. So now, I purpose to never again forget you, in my prayers and in my actions.

Please remember me in your prayers as I will remember you in mine.

Blessings in Christ,

Ken

◆ ◆ ◆

God never forgets His own

Moses recorded one of the most profound of all of God's truths in Deuteronomy 31:6; "Be strong and of good courage, do not fear nor be afraid of them; for the LORD your God, He is the One who goes with you. He will not leave you nor forsake you."

The writer to the Hebrews expanded on this when he wrote in Hebrews 13:5-6; "Let your conduct be without covetousness; be content with such things as you have. For He Himself has said, 'I will never leave you nor forsake you.' So we may boldly say: 'The Lord is my helper; I will not fear. What can man do to me?'"

Humans, Christians too, are prone to differing forms of self-imprisonment - from fear and anxiety to immorality and selfishness. God never forgets nor forsakes the Christian believer, no matter the nature of his or her imprisonment or personal trial. Whether behind concrete and steel walls of a manmade prison, or spiritual walls erected by stress, depression, disease or sin, God never forgets His own. Temporal and eternal freedom lays waiting for the one who embraces the truth of God's undying love and forgiveness.

Call on Him. He has never forgotten your name.

Letter Two:
The Rehab of Rahab

Hebrews 11:31

"By faith the prostitute Rahab, because she welcomed the spies, was not killed with those who were disobedient."

Ken,

You asked me to share from the confines of prison some thoughts gleaned from my experiences while incarcerated.

My mind goes to a most unlikely heroine in Joshua's holy war to take the Holy Land. When Joshua "fit da battle of Jericho, And da walls came tumblin' down," one house remained unscathed. It was the house with a scarlet ribbon signaling amnesty for a woman named Rahab.

In the Hebrew way of thinking it was most improbable that this person could be viewed as a champion: She was a woman, she was not of the tribe of Israel, she was in the enemy camp and she was a whore. Yet in the New Testament, Rahab is more noteworthy than any other female character of the Old Testament. She is cast in the limelight of Jesus' genealogy (Matt. 1); she made the Hall of Faith in Hebrews 11; and she is praised as an example of true faith in James 2.

In our world filled with shocking news of hate and crime, theories of punishment and rehabilitation abound. As I live, walk and breathe the same air as many men convicted of various crimes, I wonder if the rehab of Rahab has an answer for us.

Rahab was a sinner, enemy, outcast to be shunned by the "chosen people." Yet thrown into the heat of the moment, at the risk of her own life, Rahab saved the two spies. What was it? Faith!

Faith comes by hearing. Rahab said, "We have heard how the Lord dried up the water of the Red Sea…for the Lord your God is God in heaven above and on the earth below…" (Joshua 2:10-11)

I have discovered that the rehab of Rahab is the rehab of rebels today. The sinner, enemy, outcast criminal element shunned by "law abiding" citizens can truly be changed by the Word of God into men of faith. I have seen some very unlikely men become heroes of faith in here.

The rehab of Rahab gives me energy to share the word of Law and Gospel in here. The rehab of Rahab gives me confidence that the Lord will use me mightily in the most unlikely of circumstances. The rehab of Rahab gives me hope that I, myself, will be restored someday to my people.

After all, Joshua 6:25 says this rehabilitated Rahab, "…lives among the Israelites to this day."

So Ken, I'll uphold the Lord and His Word in here, then hang a scarlet rope out my window awaiting the mercy and deliverance of the Lord when the walls of prison come tumblin' down.

In His hands,

Tom

◆ ◆ ◆

Tom,

Your letter regarding Rahab really touches the heart of our faith. It speaks to all of us, to the one who is still a Rahab and to the one who is set free by the blood of Christ.

Yes, Tom, you are a Rahab languishing behind the walls of prison, and in many ways so am I behind the brooding walls of self-pity. For prison walls are made of many different kinds of materials, including paralyzing attitudes.

For a time Rahab remained free even while held captive by Jericho's unbelief, but in time, God worked to set her free to live as part of the family of Israel. So you remain free inside the prison, though held captive by the state, awaiting God's sure deliverance.

I looked at Hebrews 11:31 again and saw that Rahab's story has a lot to teach us today. I see myself too often from the perspective of standing outside the prison walls of sin, wanting more and more to climb over to higher and higher positions in the church, then feeling sorry for myself because I haven't attained it and thereby forgetting Rahab's humble role. This view contributes to my tendency to be indifferent to others' plight.

The greatness of Israel, though, is found in the fall of the walls of Jericho. Our modern faith is tested by really believing that those walls fell without the use of visible force-we look for a natural cause, or to man's obedience. They fell only by God's grace and mercy, which produced an even greater obedience and strength in the hearts of the Israelites.

Israel demonstrated her faith by walking around the city day after day. What makes this so remarkable is that nowhere in the promise to Joshua did God mention how long it would take for the walls to fall. We might conclude that Israel thought the walls would fall on the first day, but they didn't. That Israel did not give up marching around the walls each day is beyond human reason. They persevered in their faith that God would keep His promise to them, and He did.

Now, this is what I think: I think of three words: faith, time, and freedom.

God has witnessed your faith in Christ and sees your scarlet ribbon from afar; it is the way of escape.

Your time of incarceration did not end in the first year, or the third, and has stretched beyond what any of us had hoped; but soon it may come to term.

Your faith keeps you in submission to the promise and that frees you during your time behind walls. Tom, the Lord continues to use you right now and He will more fully use you when His "time" breaks down the physical prison walls that surround you. Then, as with Rahab, you will be set free to serve Him and He will use you to build His Church.

Together, let us keep marching around the walls of our own Jericho's and watch as God brings them down, and sets us free.

In God's grace,

Ken

◆ ◆ ◆

Faith on display

"Even so let your light shine before men; that they may see your good works, and glorify your Father who is in heaven." (Matthew 5:16)

God spoke by His Word in ways that cannot be dismissed. He asks us to have living faith, observable faith, no matter what walled city in which we live, our personal Jerichos.

Rahab lived in a terrible place and had a despicable occupation. She saw the light of God in the obedience of His people, and it drew her to faith. Her faith set her apart in a mean, treacherous world, but she held to it and then put it on display.

You might live behind prison walls of bricks, bars and mortar, or on the outside, behind walls created by hypocrisy, self-centeredness and fear. Now is the time to let your faith be seen.

God sees your heart. But does the world see your scarlet ribbon of faith, or have you hidden it behind the walls of your Jericho? Have you been judged as too sinful by the court of men to receive forgiveness? Have you judged yourself as beyond rehabilitation?

God set Rahab free and used her to bless His people. You, too, can be set free.

God said He would deliver those who confess faith in Him. Then confess your faith in Him, and let your faith hang on public display. Then watch as God delivers you from your own Jericho.

Letter Three:
Full of Meanness or Meaningfulness

Genesis 39:20-40:4

"And Joseph's master took him, and put him into the prison, a place where the king's prisoners were bound: and he was there in the prison. But the LORD was with Joseph, and showed him mercy, and gave him favor in the sight of the keeper of the prison. And the keeper of the prison committed to Joseph's hand all the prisoners that were in the prison; and whatsoever they did there, he was the doer of it . The keeper of the prison looked not to any thing that was under his hand; because the LORD was with him, and that which he did, the LORD made it to prosper.

"And it came to pass after these things, that the butler of the king of Egypt and his baker had offended their lord the king of Egypt. And Pharaoh was wroth against two of his officers, against the chief of the butlers, and against the chief of the bakers. And he put them in ward in the house of the captain of the guard, into the prison, the place where Joseph was bound. And the captain of the guard charged Joseph with them, and he served them: and they continued a season in ward."

Ken,

We find these words recorded in Genesis 39:20 and 40:4: "Joseph's master took him and put him in prison

...[later]...Pharaoh...put the chief cupbearer and the chief baker in custody...in the same prison where Joseph was confined...The captain of the guard assigned them to Joseph and he attended them."

The thing about prison is that you don't have many choices. And the choices you have become very crucial to well-being and even survival.

Having been falsely accused and wrongly convicted and sent to prison, I found myself in the difficult position of choice. My human nature desired to go the route of bitterness and anger. The nature of Christ in me, however, sought for God's divine purpose. Therefore, it was either seek to be full of meanness or meaningfulness.

Joseph's example in the Egyptian prison was one of seeking meaningfulness. God granted him success in whatever he did (Gen. 39:23) and Joseph humbly attended to the needs of fellow inmates. In the same way, to a lesser degree, the Lord has granted me success in a meaningful way.

I'll share with you about Mark who had changed in his 24 years of prison from a tall, bushy-haired, energetic convict activist to an emaciated, stooped, cane-supported, thin gray-haired "old-timer" ravaged by the consequences of his past life. Mark once said to me, "I know you are a preacher but I see you're all right, so I won't hold that against you."

I had known Mark for 15 years of my incarceration. Years ago we had a secret "prison clerk's union." He was clerk in the laundry, I was clerk in the kitchen. Others of the union worked in different departments. We took care of one another. But this fall, due to an early life of drug usage, Mark suffered from acute Hepatitis. His liver and kidneys were mush.

Mark hobbled up to me in the living unit commons in September and said, "The doctor says I'm dying and I won't make it to the new century. I'd really like to come to hear your Bible study sometime." Mark didn't make it to my Bible study-he had to be taken to surgery, then confined to the Maximum Security clinic to linger until his death.

I commend the prison mental health department for recognizing that a man in prison should not die deserted in the solitude of a prison infirmary. Mental health developed a hospice program. Mark requested that I visit him even though I am in a medium security unit and he was in the "max." The mental health people interviewed me and the prison security internal investigation unit cleared me. I was able to set a schedule to visit Mark.

On the night Mark died, during the time I sat beside him, nothing highly dramatic took place. We spoke of past sins, their consequences, the way of all men, the unfailing love of God. As his lungs filled with fluid, Mark struggled for each breath while confessing his simple faith in Jesus Christ. I prayed. He said, "Amen," with a sense of finality. Nothing dramatic.

Like Joseph attended to the baker and cupbearer, I attended to Mark and angels somewhere in heaven rejoiced.

As I took the long walk back through the confines of the Maximum Security Unit, I felt a comforting sense of freedom that comes from setting aside meanness for meaningfulness. Mark was free and with his freedom I, too, was released.

In Christ,

Tom

◆ ◆ ◆

Tom,

As I read your letter about "Meanness," I realize there is meanness in all of us. I know there is in me. But in Christ, we can channel meanness into meaningfulness - the meaningfulness of saving souls through the spoken Word. This is what you did when you comforted Mark through his confession and Christ's absolution, and it is a message available to all people.

There is something else in your letter that struck me. You wrote, "Now I commend the prison mental health department for recognizing that a man in prison should not die deserted in the solitude of a prison infirmary. The mental health people interviewed me and the prison security internal investigation unit cleared me. I was able to set a schedule to visit Mark."

What struck me are the methods God often uses to replicate His kindness. In Gen. 39:20 and 40:4, we read of Potiphar putting Joseph in prison and then Pharaoh putting the chief cupbearer and the chief baker into the same prison. Thereupon, the captain of the guard assigned these men to Joseph. This was no mere coincidence. This was a wonderful work of God and He used Joseph to deliver His grace.

We know that the Lord converts to peace those who are His enemies and enemies of each other, and since the ways of Joseph were pleasing to God, He used Joseph to bring His Word to these men - even though no record exists that they were all converted.

I see a parallel here. This kindness on the part of the captain (the mental health department) arose, I believe, from the fact that the Lord was with you (Gen. 39:2). And you brought to Mark the saving Gospel of Jesus Christ. You left him with a word of forgiveness that declared him righteous in the eyes of God. He left this world from a prison hospice and entered by faith into Christ's eternity. Wisdom spoke through a modern-day Joseph - Tom Bird.

Martin Luther thought of Joseph when he read from the Book of Wisdom 10:13-14, "When a righteous man was sold, wisdom did not desert him but delivered him from sin. She descended with him into the dungeon, and when he was in prison, she did not leave him, until she brought him the scepter of a kingdom and authority over his masters." Luther cherished this passage because it characterized Joseph's protection of wisdom. The Son of God, who is Wisdom, and who was to become incarnate, was with Joseph and Joseph was with Him.

Wisdom, who became man in Christ Jesus, is with you, Tom, and I know that you are with Him also. He will, in His time, obtain release for you. He has already given you release from this earthly vessel and pledged His eternal presence to you on the day you enter Christ's eternity.

So, my dear friend, reflect daily on this: Wisdom descended with you into the dungeon, and though in prison, she will not leave you, until she sets you free and unites you with your beloved wife Terry. These, I believe, are divine works, and they remind us to remain patient and faithful during trials of every kind.

Christ uses each of us who are willing to serve Him in any situation, to create meaning in each of our actions. Thank you for this reminder for me. And remember, your life has meaning, and your ministry in captivity is meaningful.

In Christ,

Ken

◆ ◆ ◆

Choose to live above evil circumstances

The Psalmist asked one of the most profound questions about how to live life, no matter what circumstances surround us. Ps. 34:12-15; "Who is the man who desires life, and loves many days, that he may see good? Keep your tongue from evil, and your lips from speaking deceit. Depart from evil and do good; seek peace and pursue it. The eyes of the LORD are on the righteous, and His ears are open to their cry."

When faced with the choice to do evil-to be mean-choose instead to hold your tongue, refrain from lies. Run from evil and instead, watch for opportunities to do good. Seek peace with all people; in fact, pursue it. The God of creation watches your works and hears your cries. And He promised to deliver you from evil. It is your choice.

The book of Hebrews reminds us about the power to choose how to live. Hebrews 9:14; "...how much more shall the blood of Christ, who through the eternal Spirit offered Himself without spot to God, cleanse your conscience from dead works to serve the living God?"

Dead evil works that bring forth death will no longer hold your conscience captive if you by faith, claim the blood of Christ; if you by faith, respond to the Holy Spirit's call to obedience; if you by faith, set aside your mean and evil nature to pursue righteousness in the power of Christ.

By trusting in the blood of Christ and the power of the Holy Spirit, you can choose to live above your evil circumstances.
God will bring good from it. As Paul wrote in Romans 8:28; "And we know that all things work together for good to those who love God, to those who are the called according to His purpose." God will use your worst circumstances to work His righteousness in and through you.

Letter Four:
Birdicus

Proverbs 17:15

"Acquitting the guilty and condemning the innocent — the Lord detests them both."

Ken,

You wondered about work in prison. After so many years in prison doing a variety of jobs, I'm blessed to have a job while incarcerated that is productive. Time goes by faster, and I have a sense of purpose. It is a blessing to have good bosses, too. My employers are not all about money and production. They are generous men and exhibit a profound sense of humor, which is essential for prison life.

The other day, sitting in the production office, my boss was perusing the synopsis of Dave Racer's book. He said, "This ruins my dream."

The office personnel smiled, anticipating a punch line - "I was going to write your story, Tom. Actually, a screen play to be made into an epic motion picture."

"Yeah, right," scoffed one of the clerks.

"Really. I was going to call it," he said while making the shape of a marquee sign with his arms, "Birdicus."

Everyone chuckled at his play on the classic epic, Spartacus. In animated fashion he continued, "Can you imagine just like the famous scene where the Romans win the battle and the rebellious slaves as prisoners sat covering the hills? The Roman Commander says, 'Give me Spartacus and I'll spare your lives.' "

We nodded in recognition of the scene and one of the sales reps interjected, "So in your version, everyone stands up and says, 'I'm Birdicus; I'm Birdicus.' "

Everyone laughed.

At that very moment that the office was close to an uproar on the spoof, suddenly, drastically, seriously, my boss leaned into the office group and with grand vision in his eyes proclaimed, "No, in this movie all those men covering the hillside would one by one rise and say, 'It could happen to me! It could happen to me!' " With the office personnel in contemplation, he withdrew out of the door, echoing, "It could happen to any of us!"

Yes, Ken, my boss has a good sense of humor and a good sense of the case. At the time he left, I turned to my desk work and there to my amazement was the Franklin Planner, "Thought for the day for November 11, 1999." It said, "Injustice anywhere is a threat to justice everywhere." Marquis de Vauvenargues.

Your friend in Christ,

Tom

◆ ◆ ◆

Tom,

Your work in prison is, indeed, a blessing from the Lord - for me too. I also sense that your co-workers find in you a "peculiar" kind of power that they have rarely, if at all, experienced in prison, or anywhere, for that matter. Peculiar because the real power is the power that God has given to His Church on earth, hence, to you - a power to preach the Word of God, to forgive and retain sins and, to open the gates of heaven in the name of Jesus.

Ironic, isn't it that we should find joy in work and detest the work that attempts to merit grace. Christ has done the work for us. He completed that work when He said on the cross, "It is finished!"

Our forgiveness is secured. We never have to work again for our salvation for He is our work and our rest; He has set us free to live in freedom and to rest in Him.

The fun your co-workers had in comparing your story to Spartacus is apt in many ways. The cry "Birdicus, Birdicus," of course, is a play on the cry "Spartacus, Spartacus" that Kirk Douglas made famous in the movie. But "Birdicus, Birdicus" means more; much more.

To me, it means BIRD-In-Christ-and-Christ-in-US. Dave Racer's book, *Caged Bird*, points out that during the ordeal leading up and including your trials, Bird was in Christ and Christ was in Bird, and the same is true during your imprisonment. And along with other facts of the criminal case, the reader will understand how the judicial system disposed itself to fail. Hopefully, the reader will cry out for justice.

I think that justice requires that we all stand up for each other as Justicus-JUST-In-Christ for-US. For when we believe that God is reconciled and favorably inclined to us because of Christ, this personal faith obtains the forgiveness of sins and justifies us. It is His work in us and for our benefit.

Your selection of Proverbs 17:15, "Acquitting the guilty and condemning the innocent, the Lord detests them both," really says it all. So often, the innocent seems to lose out, while the criminal with the best attorney gets away with murder.

The celebrated attorney Clarence Darrow once said, "There is no such thing as justice - in or out of court." And, so it often appears. But God takes note, and does not forget. And He has not forgotten us either.

Yes, your boss was right when he said, "It could happen to me!" Yes, "It could happen to any of us!"

You quoted Marquis de Vauvenargues who said, "Injustice anywhere is a threat to justice everywhere," and I wondered if he had not thought of Isaiah's words: "Woe to those who drag iniquity with the cord of falsehood and take away the rights of the ones who are in the right." (Isaiah 5:18,23). This, too, is an abomination to the Lord.

So let me join the choir and sing Birdicus, Birdicus and add the refrain Justicus, Justicus-justice in Christ for us. For we who believe in Christ possess what He offered and promised — faith, forgiveness, peace, love and the hope of eternal life.

The end of the matter is that we who have faith in Christ are truly free.

Benefits my brother,

Ken

◆ ◆ ◆

Set free though guilty

"But I'm innocent," many criminal defendants claim, and some really are innocent, even though a jury condemns them to prison. The movie *Innocent Victims* portrays one such true case in which a man on death row won a new trial, and once there, a jury found him not guilty; actually they found him innocent.

Most of us believe that our justice system always renders a fair verdict. If anything, we believe that too many guilty persons go free. As well, we believe that we will never be the defendant in a criminal case, because we have put our faith in the law.

As it concerns what really matters, our Heavenly Judge sees things differently for those who live in self-sufficiency. Paul wrote in Romans 3:23, "For all have sinned and come short of the glory of God," and in Romans 6:23, "For the wages of sin is death, but the gift of God is eternal life through Jesus Christ our Lord."

What really matters is eternity. Though we are guilty as charged, or wrongfully charged and convicted, God placed our violations on Jesus Christ who took our blame and our penalty. Paul wrote in Romans 10:9-11, "...that if you confess with your mouth the Lord Jesus and believe in your heart that God has raised Him from the dead, you will be saved. For with the heart one believes unto righteousness, and with the mouth confession is made unto salvation."

None of us can be sure that we will not be wrongfully accused by human prosecutors. Having been so accused, our fate lies in the hands of an imperfect human jury. Found guilty even though innocent, we will still go to prison.

All of us can be sure that we stand rightfully accused by Almighty God. Having been so accused, we can be secure knowing that our eternal fate rests in the hands of a perfect Savior, Jesus Christ. Found innocent even though guilty, we are set free.

Letter five:
Escapades of Escape

1 Corinthians 10:13

"There hath no temptation taken you but such as man can bear: but God is faithful, who will not suffer you to be tempted above that ye are able; but will with the temptation make also the way of escape, that ye may be able to endure it." (1 Corinthians 10:13)

Ken,

Freedom, my good friend, is a potent desire of all men to be able to move, act and experience life without shackles or restraints. Escape, Ken, is a natural consideration for any man who has had such liberty wrested from him.

The seeds of an escape plot used to often tantalize my mind in my earlier years of incarceration. Why wouldn't it? Wrongly convicted, sentenced to possible life imprisonment, continually disappointed by the failures of the justice system to come to grips with strong points of appeal and overwhelming new evidence in my case. Escape! Yes, it is a thought.

Hey, Ken, I saw the movie, "The Fugitive," a popular flick. You and millions of others plopped down 10 bucks to cheer for the escapee. How about the academy award winning "Shawshank Redemption?" Millions certainly felt it was money well spent to experience gratification with this justice turned upside down saga of escape (note that both were wrongly convicted of murdering their wives). What many on the outside enjoyed as a movie, I relished as a challenging fantasy — escape. I guess it's a matter of perspective.

Let's talk about perspective.

Think of this, Ken: If people were willing to drop $20 or $30 to be satisfied watching from a theater seat a couple "righteous escapees" from prison, how much more satisfying would it be to send a few dollars to actually help a person in real life win a "righteous freedom" from prison?

In my latter years here I think a lot more about escape. But it is a different kind of escape. You see, I found where God promised to aid and abet my escape. It is tempting to think about busting out of this joint; but it would be wrong. The "powers to be are ordained of God (Romans 13)." So the escape I have learned to contemplate is the escape Paul talks of in I Corinthians 10:13: "…God will with the temptation also make a way to escape, that ye may be able to bear it."

I sin sometimes. I am tempted by bitterness, anger and worry. Then my mind turns to the truth that God is faithful - He provides an escape from every temptation. He knows what I am able to withstand more than I. He protects me this way. When tempted, the Lord intervenes with the promise that He will provide a way to escape. When I fail, I am driven to the cross in repentance for Christ's sake to receive forgiveness.

Yes, Ken, I think about escape a lot. I think about a faithful Lord who provides my escape from sin. What a blessing!

Tom

◆ ◆ ◆

Tom,

Oh yes, freedom is precious, especially when you don't have it.

Your letter on escape brought back some painful memories in my own life, although they can hardly be compared to yours.

In 1967, I joined the army for fear of being drafted and sent to Vietnam. When I arrived at Fort Campbell, Kentucky, my life literally belonged to the Drill Instructor; he kept me and all the other troops in his control night and day for three months.

I felt like I was in a closet and could not get out. I wanted to run away, escape from my responsibilities as a soldier but I couldn't. If I did, I would have been absent without leave (AWOL) and if caught, thrown in the brig. Fear of disgrace caused me to pause. Fear of God compelled me to stay. The love of Christ inspired me to endure.

I believed, and still do, that God would not allow me to be pressured beyond my ability to withstand, that He would give me the wherewithal I needed to see it through. And by His grace, He did.

I did not have a life sentence to suffer; just three years of army life apart from my Katherine. I saw the approaching reality of fighting in war. Then with just eight months left in service, Uncle Sam gave me orders to report to Da Nang, South Vietnam.

I had thought that by enlisting, I could avoid Vietnam, but my plan didn't work my way. The army had different plans.

Still, I was not wrongfully convicted and I didn't spend a large portion of my life incarcerated. I volunteered, and resolved to do my duty, such as is common to all soldiers. I had no excuse and no escape.

I did my three years, and now when I look back I must say that they were good years.

I watched both the "Fugitive" and "Shawshank Redemption," and immediately thought of your anguish. Yes, these movies do have a way of stirring up the emotions and moving people to action. I can only pray that Dave Racer's book *Caged Bird* will bring hope to you and a new trial.

Tom, I looked again at 1 Cor. 10:13: "No temptation has seized you except what is common to man. And God is faithful; he will not let you be tempted beyond what you can bear. But when you are tempted, he will also provide a way out so that you can stand up under it."

That little phrase, "but God is faithful," is pure Gospel. The Corinthians cleaved to God, not to themselves for escape from the dangers that followed temptation. And God is trustworthy as is proved by the way He controls temptation. He does not allow us to be tempted above our ability; He makes a way out through our ability.

Even for the saints it is hard to endure, but our hearts believe it because the Holy Spirit convinces us in the Word that God wills us to be faithful. And so we have a faithful and gracious God because of Christ.

"God sent the Son into the world, not to condemn the world, but that the world might be saved through him. He who believes in him is not condemned." (John 3:17f).

Enduring temptation by the power of Christ, whether the temptation is to try to escape from prison, to escape from our responsibilities, or escape from the prison of sin, is overcome by the power of Christ.

God is Faithful,

Ken

◆ ◆ ◆

Our eternal escape is assured

"You are of God, little children, and have overcome them: because He who is in you is greater than he who is in the world." (1 John 4:4)

Few of us sit behind rigid stone walls or barb-wired topped chain link fence. We do not dream of breaking through, climbing over or digging under such barriers. But often we are incarcerated behind other walls of our own making, or barriers built by Satan and his minions.

We want to escape from marriage, or parenthood (or the restrictions of childhood), or an unjust employer. We want to run away from responsibilities. We view them as walls holding us captive.

More than two million Americans sit behind cold prison walls. Their daily walk is limited to a few square blocks, and only when the jailer gives permission. Most long for freedom. Giving in to hopelessness is an option that daily stares them in the face.

Satan shows us images or situations and we feel an urge to surrender to sin. Sinfulness springs forth from our hearts like a well of putrid water threatening to flood over us. We feel as though we may sink into the heavy clay of sin.

We earnestly desire to escape these temptations.

Our escape is assured, because God is greater than all our temptations. No walls can hold our spirit in bondage when His Spirit has set us free.

Submit all your temptations to His care, and He will deliver you to true freedom.

"Draw nigh to God, and he will draw nigh to you." (James 4:8a)

Letter Six:
Pomp and Circumstantial Evidence

Genesis 44:14ff

Ken,

Today's letter is not from a modern day Joseph. This is a page from a modern day Benjamin. Go with me on this thought for a minute.

The story of Joseph is truly a magnificent saga of God's providence. We follow Joseph after he was released. He went from prison to palace - second in command of all Egypt. He was delivered from pauper to prince after a shower, shave and new suit (Genesis 41:14, 41).

Joseph was a powerful man and with it came all the pomp and circumstance. When Joseph traveled in his chariot the entourage before him cleared the path shouting, "Make way!" (Genesis 41:43)

Those who were brought into his presence would "bow down faces to the ground." (Genesis 41:44)

What did Joseph do with his pomp and power? He saved many all over the known world from death by famine. This included his brothers who were the ones that sold him into slavery. But torn with emotions, Joseph determined to test his brothers before they found out who he really was.

After buying grain on their second journey, Joseph had his silver cup planted in the saddlebag of the youngest brother Benjamin.

After the brothers left Egypt, they were tracked down.

Confident of their innocence, the brothers said, search our bags; if anyone is found with the cup, he will die and the rest will be your slaves (there were no Miranda Rights protection in that day, no Fifth Amendment right against self-incrimination and no constitutional guard against illegal search and seizure). But, Ken, when a person is innocent, he doesn't need those rights, does he? Wrong! So wrong!

The brothers said, "Here, search our bags."

The palace servant found Joseph's silver cup in Benjamin's bag. Benjamin was arrested. All the brothers came back to Joseph. Judah, spokesman and advocate for the brothers pleaded with two very significant questions: "What can we say? How can we prove our innocence?" (Genesis 44:16)

The pomp of the second in command of Egypt and the circumstantial evidence of the cup in his saddlebag had nailed Benjamin. How can he prove his innocence?

I'm sure that Joseph, during his years of imprisonment, often asked, "How can I prove my innocence to Potiphar?" He, too, was found guilty by the pomp and circumstantial evidence of the coat in Potiphar's wife's hand.

Oh, how I identify with Benjamin here! In my years of imprisonment, I have pleaded like Judah - what can I say? How can I prove my innocence? A pompous press and circumstantial evidence convicted me in Kansas.

The Lord vindicated Joseph; the Lord vindicated Benjamin; and, Ken, I have faith that the Lord will vindicate me. "What can I say? How can I prove my innocence?"

After tons of research, Dave Racer is on the brink of answering those questions when the book is published.

Peace be with you,

Tom

Tom,

I thought of the Apostle Peter as I read your letter and the agonizing question you proposed, "What can I say?" For your life during these past years has been an example of what Peter encouraged: "For it is commendable if a man bears up under the pain of unjust suffering because he is conscious of God." (1 Peter 2:19)

I have often asked, "What does God want me to do?"

Although we are constantly stressed by temptations, few of us are asked to bear suffering wrongfully, as you have been forced to do. I recall my childhood when my father reminded me that punishment would be mine for my wrongdoing. I also learned that when I did not do some wrong I loudly objected to any form or threat of punishment. Then I spoke up, proclaiming my innocence, because I believed that I should not suffer for things I did not do. But this kind of suffering is so unlike yours.

We know the world cares little about whether suffering is just. It is often unfair. This evil world often punishes unjustly.

Judges and prosecutors are not always interested in truth and justice; sometimes they are more interested in conviction and sentencing. These latter look good on their record showing they are "tough on crime."

I wonder how many innocent people are incarcerated because the "tough on crime" sentiment can obscure the principle of reasonable doubt? How often does that sentiment do damage to truth and justice?

When I see situations of wrongful conviction I cry, "It isn't right! What has this person done to deserve this?" Still, it is clear that innocent men, including Christians, are thus punished. Why? The Apostle Peter says that it is because we are "conscious of God." That is, we want to serve Him in all we do. We want to work for our spiritual rewards. We want to show love by restraining ourselves toward those who wish to harm us. And that, Tom, is exactly what you have been doing.

"What can I say?" you ask?

Let me tell you.

In all these years of suffering, I have heard you speak the truth in regard to your sad situation. These truths have been verified by Dave Racer and shown plainly in *Caged Bird*. But there is more here, and it accrues to your faith.

It is what you do not say that speaks loudly about true faith. I have never heard you speak ill of anyone, not even those who are your earthly enemies, those who wrongfully convicted you. I have never seen or sensed anger or hatred in your speech or your letters directed at them. On the contrary, when I get mad at the false and misleading testimony your detractors gave in court, you have always put the best construction on their words so as to see what was really said. This forces me to look deeper into your case and into my own heart.

Whenever the world makes us suffer for doing what God wants us to do, it is showing its true colors. The world is contrary to God, contrary to real happiness, contrary to righteousness.

When we ask what God would have us do and actually do it, we are showing that the Holy Spirit is dwelling within us. We are showing that God is our Lord. Such a witness is bound to cause us discomfort in this life. All such discomfort is short and insignificant when we see the glory that will be revealed to us in heaven.

Our Lord promotes us. He gives recognition. He commends us. He protects us. He sets us free.

Blessings in Christ,

Ken

◆ ◆ ◆

So what if it is not your fault?

"And who is he who will harm you if you become followers of what is good? But even if you should suffer for righteousness' sake, you are blessed. And do not be afraid of their threats, nor be troubled. But sanctify the Lord God in your hearts, and always be ready to give a defense to everyone who asks you a reason for the hope that is in you, with meekness and fear; having a good conscience, that when they defame you as evildoers, those who revile your good conduct in Christ may be ashamed. For it is better, if it is the will of God, to suffer for doing good than for doing evil. For Christ also suffered once for sins, the just for the unjust, that He might bring us to God, being put to death in the flesh but made alive by the Spirit..." (1 Peter 3:13-18)

God looks upon the heart. He searches out intentions. He also sees our actions, and so does the world.

God uses the actions of a person rightly motivated to draw people to Himself. And that testimony can be even greater if we are willing to act righteously even when wrongfully accused.

Yet, how many of us are condemned even though guiltless? If we are punished because we are guilty, then we have no standing to complain about conviction. Still, even when rightfully convicted we have the same opportunity as the innocent man.

Man may punish us regardless of our guilt or innocence, but God rewards us with his grace and mercy, and with the gift of faith. And it is this gift of faith that moves us to obedience, no matter how, when, why or by whom we are persecuted.

You have no control over how others will treat you, so what does it matter? With the Holy Spirit's help, you can, out of a good conscience, do the right thing.

Set your heart on doing what is right and rise above your circumstances.

Letter Seven:
"Brothers & Cisterns"

Genesis 37:21

Dear Ebed-Melech,

I won't address you as "Ken" today. For today, I'll call you "Ebed-Melech." You'll see why.

Joseph's brothers wanted to kill him for unjust reasons. Yet, unwilling to have the blood of a brother on their hands, they threw him into an empty cistern. (Genesis 37:24)

This was not the only time someone was unjustly thrown into a cistern.

Recorded in Jeremiah 38, King Zedekiah's officials were afraid of Jeremiah and did not like his prophecy against Jerusalem. They wanted to kill him; but fearing to have the blood of a prophet on their hands, they opted to lower Jeremiah into a cistern where he "sank down into the mud." (Jeremiah 38:6) There he would starve to death. The king, though in charge of justice in the city, allowed this to happen.

Now, it was not the best of times for people of Jerusalem. The Babylonian army had surrounded the city. People were discouraged, hungry and panicky. Anyone remotely connected to the king's palace would be put to death or carted off as servants to Babylon.

In this darkest moment of Jerusalem, there arose a man named Ebed-Melech, a minor court official in King Zedekiah's palace. Ebed-Melech put aside all his personal cares and worries. He boldly went forward to the king and declared, "My lord the king, these men acted wickedly in all they have done to Jeremiah the prophet." (Jeremiah 38:9)

The king, struck by the caring concern of Ebed-Melech, told him, "Lift Jeremiah out of the cistern before he dies."

Risking their own lives, Ebed and 30 men came to the dramatic rescue.

Even though Jeremiah was an inspired prophet of God, we cannot sell short the depth of his human suffering. Jeremiah was living in mud and darkness. Can you imagine the joy and vitality he felt when that rescue rope dropped to him from Ebed?

Ken, where the courts and justice system has failed me, you have dropped a rope and lifted me up. No, I am not literally sunken in mud or starving; but I am mired in the system and languishing through so many years of imprisonment. It is truly a joy to look up from the bottom of this cistern where I live and see you.

It's not you alone, either.

As Ebed gathered 30 men to make this dramatic rescue, so I have been blessed with hundreds who are supporting and participating in my deliverance: My wife, Terry; my father; family; friends and many I do not even know.

Oh that there were more Ebed-Melech's in our modern day Christian churches!

The Lord is pleased with His people who set aside all their problems to take an opportunity to help others in need. Ebed-Melech was blessed for his saving of Jeremiah. When Jerusalem fell and all the people were being captured or killed, the Lord said to Ebed, "I will save you, you will not fall by the sword but will escape with your life because you trust in me." (Jeremiah 39:18)

Ken, you are my Ebed-Melech, which in Hebrew means, "King's servant." You certainly are a servant of Christ, our King. I am grateful!

Tom

◆ ◆ ◆

Tom,

Your letter today overwhelms me. I am not used to hearing compliments and I am not good at receiving them. Like many people, I usually make light of compliments and then quickly change the subject. My discomfort makes it difficult to know what to say. Receiving a compliment points to my inadequacies. I feel that I should give it rather than receive it.

But thank you dear brother for thinking of me while you are in the pit, even as I am free and enjoying life.

I really never paid much attention to Ebed-Melech before, but now I am interested in knowing more about him. So I looked him up in Jeremiah 38. I see that he was a Cushite and that, I suppose, makes him a black man.

Ebed-Melech's race and ministration to Jeremiah stimulated a whole line of thinking. His story touched on a personal and cultural level because my son-in-law, James Weston, is African-American. I have had the distinct privilege of baptizing and then marrying James to my daughter Naomi, and I love him deeply.

This caused me to reflect on the blessings of baptism and sanctity of marriage. Remember what we were taught in seminary? Baptism works forgiveness of sins, delivers from death and the devil, and gives eternal salvation to all who believe.

Marriage requires that we love and honor our spouses. This sends a message to all of us.

I wonder how many people know of the essential work that you and Terry have done in your marriage enrichment seminars there in prison. Surely, the Lord is pleased with your work; God has been glorified, even as those married couples have been blessed.

James and Naomi have three wonderful little children: Olivia, Isaiah, and Sophia. Olivia spends Tuesday mornings with me as I lead the ladies' Bible study. Afterwards, I take her to lunch. We say our prayers, we eat, and she plays with other children and does most of the talking. Then I take her home and kiss her good-bye. She is my darling and we have a blessed time.

There I go again, getting off the story of Ebed-Melech. I see that he took 30 men with him, but not because they would all be necessary for getting Jeremiah out of the pit. He wanted to make sure that his effort would result in releasing the prophet. He knew that attempts would be made by the princes and the people to stop him.

Tom, the princes and the populace of Emporia failed you and wrongfully threw you into a pit. It is a black mark on them and on the justice system. The ultimate black mark, though, is on your name and your innocence. Truly, 30 "men" - Terry, your mom and dad, brother Mark and sister Gloria, Herman Otten, Dave Racer and others - are still working and giving faithful attention to create a rope of freedom to pull you out of your pit. But much remains to be done.

The Cushite King finally allowed Jeremiah to be pulled out of his pit. The 30 "men" with me continue to try to convince the Kansas "King" to allow you the same freedom. If you must call me Ebed-Melech, then I will pledge this: this Cushite will continue to do all I can to lower the rope of freedom to your hands.

As you are grateful for help so we are thankful to offer it. As you are blessed in your daily walk with God so we all see that God's grace in Christ will never cease to reach out to you with His love and careful attention.

Let us pray together that God will send more Ebed-Melech's to the side of others, like you, who have been wrongfully convicted, or who have lost position due to the fear and jealousy of others. And in the same way, let us pray that God's people will answer His call to minister to those in prison, even those who deserve to be there.

I am grateful and blessed, too, that God has given to you the wherewithal to do his work in the "pit" as I do mine in the parish.

Blessings my brother,

Ken

◆ ◆ ◆

Those in the pits

We have all lived in the miry clay of sin, depression and defeat. Our guilt condemns us. And others have often wrongfully accused and judged us guilty for our actions. We even wrongfully judge and condemn ourselves.

We rejoice when God sends someone to rescue us and lift us up.

Likewise, we see others imprisoned in their own despair and dilemma. God's Spirit challenges our heart to reach out and rescue that person or that family.

Do we, as did Ebed-Melech, then take the initiative to rescue others from their own human pits of despair, defeat and depression?

But, we answer, "He deserves that punishment for his guilt. Why should I reach out to him?"

On Judgment Day, as all of mankind stands before the throne of Christ, He will separate the sheep from the goats. To those who will enter His heaven, He offers thanksgivings for their ministry to others.

Matthew 25:34-36; "Then the King will say to those on His right hand, 'Come, you blessed of My Father, inherit the kingdom prepared for you from the foundation of the world: 'for I was hungry and you gave Me food; I was thirsty and you gave Me drink; I was a stranger and you took Me in; I was naked and you clothed Me; I was sick and you visited Me; I was in prison and you came to Me.'"

As Christ commends His children for relieving others' suffering, He draws no distinction between those rightfully or wrongfully accused.

In a sense, Christ sees all true Christians as Ebed-Melech, ready to take the initiative to relieve the suffering of others, to work for earthly justice for those living in despair, oppression, sickness, alone and imprisoned.

You can be an Ebed-Melech to another person. Pray that the Holy Spirit will lay on you that desire to rescue another from the pit of despair.

Letter Eight:
My Asenath

Genesis 42:45

"Pharaoh gave (Joseph) Asenath."

Ken,

Going back to the mid-70s, I recall your lovely wife cooking a great Italian meal for Sandy and me. Within only minutes after we met that day, I know that you could tell that Sandy was a very special child of God.

To me Sandy was the ideal woman described in Proverbs 31:10-31. Verses like "she sets about her work vigorously" (v. 17) or "she looketh well to the ways of her household..." (v. 27) aptly describe Sandy. Simultaneously, she was a dedicated mother and astute college educator. I counted my life blessed to have been her husband.

Sandy lived her life to the fullest, accomplishing more in her few years than most who live twice as long. I did not take Sandy's life; but I did take her for granted. I confess that sin.

Now Joseph had no wife before prison. Nor did he have a wife while he was serving time in prison. But soon upon his release, he married a noble woman who later gave birth to two sons who each were given a portion of the Promised Land of Israel.

Here again, Ken, I find that I have been blessed by the Lord much more than Joseph. For I was astonished that God gave to me Terry in marriage while I have been in prison. There was much scoffing at a woman marrying a man doing life in prison convicted of killing his wife. Few would understand. Many would speculate. Thinking only about sex, one newspaper assumed conjugal visits were going on (not so). One reporter said Terry married me to avoid having to testify against me. Intriguing idea, but not true. In a baffled state, some concluded that the "womanizer" Bird manipulated with mind control this naïve young teacher into marriage. Makes for good soap opera; but all this is preposterous. Terry is a savvy woman with a gift of discernment. The Proverbs 31 "wife of noble character" also fits Terry very well.

Terry and I saw each other before I came to prison. She attended all my trials. We have developed an intimate relationship beyond the imagination of most people's concept of marriage. We have helped organize and attended since our August 4, 1988 wedding, more than a dozen marriage enrichment seminar weekends together. Ask any wife what value she would put on 10 hours a week of intimate conversation with her husband. That is what we have here during visiting hours at prison, frankly, because that is all we can have. But the opportunity has been great for us.

Even though Terry is a wonderful and gifted woman faithful to her Lord, she does not have an easy life. She has sacrificed a lot by her choice of marrying me. While I have been incarcerated, she has been a loving mother to my children. She has earned two master's degrees in education and fulfills the monumental task as a called teacher and administrator in our Lutheran schools. "She speaks with wisdom, and faithful instruction is on her tongue." (Proverbs 31:26) She still finds time for me and continually shores up my faith and encourages me in my small ministry here.

As Joseph was blessed with a wife upon his release from prison, I have been twice blessed by the Lord. First with Sandy, and then the Lord put my Asenath, Terry, in my life. It has been a double portion of grace given that I don't deserve. My heart does ache for Terry that she is so often alone out there and my heart longs to be with her.

Hug your wife, Ken, and God bless.

Tom

Tom,

I love remembering Seminary days. In those days, Katherine loved to make spaghetti and meatballs and lasagna for dinner guests. She made her own sauce from scratch, though now, because of busy schedules and other things she uses "store bought" sauce. It's still good though. I also remember that we always had a glass of *oinos* (wine) for everyone and dinner would never be complete without the common German elixir, Liebfraumilch. Thank you for remembering those days, Tom. They were great.

Yes, Sandy was a wonderful woman and a devoted wife. I appreciate your quotes from Proverbs about Sandy and Terry - and how well they fit. So much is said of how a wife and mother clothes her family and how important that is to everyone. Still, the real beauty of her appearance comes not from outward clothing, but from inner qualities - strength, dignity, confidence, wisdom, faithfulness, concern, and industriousness (Prov. 31:25-27).

So many modern couples try in vain to find love and satisfaction in outward appearances and possessions. They buy into the notion that outward appearance is the best way to make themselves acceptable and appealing to others. The Scriptures constantly remind us that real beauty is found in the attitude of the heart. When I think of Sandy, that is what comes to my mind - the attitude of her heart. She blessed everyone who knew her.

And Terry is a great blessing too. Over the years, I have come to know her as a compassionate, wise, strong and loving person. I am amazed at how she stands up under all the pressure of work and home without having her husband beside her every day. She simply caries on without complaint. This is a wonderful quality.

I think Verse 30 summarizes the chapter very well. Beauty is fleeting. Literally, it is a 'breath' that evaporates like a fleeting breath on a cold day. This is the same Hebrew word translated 'meaningless' in Ecc. 1:2-3. Proverbs 1:7 states, 'The fear of the Lord is the beginning of knowledge.' This is the driving force in a noble woman's life. What comes from fearing God is anything but fleeting. It lasts for a lifetime and on into eternity.

It's appropriate that Proverbs ends as it began, with the fear of God. This theme has run throughout the book. To fear God is to stand in reverent awe before him, and to love and trust in him. This is the beginning, the middle, and the end of godly wisdom.

Tom, when I got home after reading your letter, I immediately walked to Katherine and gave her a hug and kiss. Thank you for your reminder of the precious nature of a Proverbs 31 wife.

In Christ,

Ken

◆ ◆ ◆

The blessed spouse

Many incarcerated people enter prison, leaving a spouse and children behind. Some marry while they remain in prison.
The Apostle Paul writes in Ephesians 5:25, "Husbands, love your wives, even as Christ also loved the church, and gave Himself for her…"

And Paul writes in Titus 2:4, about older women, "…that they admonish the young women to love their husbands, to love their children, to be discreet, chaste, homemakers, good, obedient to their own husbands, that the word of God may not be blasphemed."

Modernists dislike these admonitions to wives and misunderstand them as male chauvinism. But Proverbs 31 shows the true honor and dignity reserved for a woman who fears God. Not only is she blessed by God, and honored by her husband, but "Her children rise up, and call her blessed…" (Prov. 31:28a)

We have such a short time on earth, but an eternity thereafter. When one spouse loses another to death, it is as if his or her own flesh has been torn apart. God may bring an "Asenath" to fill that void and along with it, renewed joy and companionship. It is the spouse He has given us now with whom we have the joy of deep communion.

Sadly, many married couples build prison walls between them, cutting off any meaningful relationship. Theirs' are walls of indifference, pride, selfishness, laziness, anger, impatience and the like - or the choice just to quit loving someone.

The incarcerated person has no control over his or her separation from a spouse.

But by God's grace, married people, no matter their situation — even when separated by prison bars — can still be united in peace, love and hope for now and eternity.

What kinds of prison bars prohibit you from deep communion with your spouse? Fear God and obey Him, and those bars fall away.

Letter Nine:
Clothes Make the Man

Genesis 37:33

"And he knew it, and said, It is my son's coat; an evil beast hath devoured him; Joseph is without doubt rent in pieces."

Ken,

Well, I lost a pair of jeans and a shirt today. They didn't return from the laundry. No big deal you might think. Except that loss amounts to 25% of my total wardrobe here in prison. You wouldn't believe the bureaucratic mumbo jumbo it takes to get another set of clothes. But really, it is no problem at all compared to Joseph's troubles with clothes.

There is a saying, "Clothes makes the man." In regard to Joseph, clothes make the story; or at least makes the story interesting.

Think about this: It was the coat of many colors that made Joseph's brothers jealous and hateful toward him. Jacob made a richly ornamental robe for Joseph. "When his brothers saw that their father loved him more than any of them, they hated him." (Gen. 37:34)

This controversial coat became planted fake "evidence" to prove to Jacob that Joseph was killed by a predator. "Then they got Joseph's robe, slaughtered a goat and dipped the robe in the blood. They took the ornamented robe back to their father and said, 'We found this'…He recognized it and said, 'It is my son's robe! Some ferocious animal has devoured him.'" (Gen. 38:21-32) [There were no DNA tests then.]

Jacob tore his clothes, put on sackcloth and mourned.

Clothes as "evidence" came into the picture again. Potiphar's wife "caught Joseph by his cloak and said, 'Come to bed with me!' But he left his cloak in her hand and ran out of the house." (Gen. 39:12) Then she accused Joseph of attempted rape, "…as soon as I screamed for help he left his cloak beside me and ran out of the house." (Gen. 39:18)

Poor Joseph! Did clothes make the man? No, clothes were used to give the man slavery and then prison.

But just as clothes played a part in Joseph's demise, clothes played a part in his restoration. When the Pharaoh pulled Joseph out of prison, he set him up as second in command. The record says that Pharaoh "dressed Joseph in robes of fine linen." (Gen. 41:42).

Years later, during the famine when Joseph revealed his identity to his brothers, clothes came as a symbol of love and reconciliation toward them. "To each of them Joseph gave new clothing…" (Gen. 45:22)

So, Ken, all these little episodes about Joseph and clothing, plus my little experience of the loss of my prison clothing in the laundry, makes me turn to thoughts of clothes of a more significant, spiritual nature. Isaiah 64:5-6 says, "…How then can we be saved? All of us have become like one who is unclean, and all our righteous acts are like filthy rags."

Here is the real spiritual wardrobe offered to us:

"Clothe yourselves with the Lord Jesus." (Romans 13:14)

"Clothe yourselves with humility." (I Peter 5:5)

"Clothe yourselves with compassion, kindness, humility, gentleness, patience." (Col 3:12)

Now these are some clothes that make the man! With this wardrobe, Ken, I can get along with three jeans and three shirts in my closet.

In Christ,

Tom

◆ ◆ ◆

Tom,

There is a lot of truth in the saying that clothes make the man, even in the church. I can remember a few years back when a District President made that very point.

With so many other pressing issues for our Missouri Synod to consider-like, creation vs. evolution, ordination of women, issues about communion, church and ministry-he chose to talk about what kind of shoes ministers should wear. Apparently, as he was going around the district he noticed that some or many of the pastors had not kept their shoes shined. He thought that shiny shoes send a message to the laity of how we see ourselves. And certainly, it is important to dress properly.

Well, we all got a big laugh out of the president's message to the church that month, but as a result, pastors did begin taking care to shine their shoes; at least, when the District President came calling.

As I thought about you losing your jeans and shirt, something else came to my mind; that seemingly small things in life take on larger meaning when they are lost.

You also made me think about how much I rely on my beloved Katherine who buys most of my clothes, if not all of them. She tells me that I have trouble putting the correct colors together, and therefore, she should handle this detail. And I can tell you that I appreciate this very much; it is not just a small thing to me.

But the real clothing behind the outside appearance you wrote about is of a higher matter, when clothing is used as evidence. We now know how the prosecutors made your "clothing" dirty with the gossip they introduced in court. For that, they and the gossipers will, in the end, have dirt on their face and character.

Still, the kind of clothing that we know of and that you wear each day is a kind that they nor anyone else can ever dirty no matter how much gossip they spread. It is the clothing of righteousness made clean by the death of Christ on the cross. The Apostle Paul, also prisoner of man and of God, tells about that kind of clothing used as evidence to one of being Christian. He writes to the Ephesian "prisoners:"

"Therefore [clothe] put on the full armor of God, so that when the day of evil comes, you may be able to stand your ground, and after you have done everything, to stand. Stand firm then, with the belt of truth buckled around your waist, with the breastplate of righteousness in place, and with your feet fitted with the readiness that comes from the gospel of peace. In addition to all this, take up the shield of faith, with which you can extinguish all the flaming arrows of the evil one. Take the helmet of salvation and the sword of the Spirit, which is the word of God. And pray in the Spirit on all occasions with all kinds of prayers and requests. With this in mind, be alert and always keep on praying for all the saints. Pray also for me, that whenever I open my mouth, words may be given me so that I will fearlessly make known the mystery of the gospel, for which I am an ambassador in chains. Pray that I may declare it fearlessly, as I should." (Eph. 6: 13-20.)

Tom, over all of these years you have been clothed with the belt, the breastplate, the shield, the helmet and the sword by Christ Himself, and He has clothed you with humility and grace. And as you have so often expressed, it is this clothing that has protected you against the worst that prison has to offer.

Blessings to you my brother,

Ken

◆ ◆ ◆

What are you wearing?

Clothing choices often evolve as a person ages.
Teens wear clothes to impress and attract their peers. Boys want to show they belong, and girls want to attract boys' attention.
College students wear clothing that often rails against tradition

and orthodoxy, to show their independence.

Younger working people wear neat and handsome clothes as they begin their careers and work to get ahead. Expectant mothers wear clothes that expand along with their stomachs.

Middle-aged people seek clothes that will hide their weight gain and sagging muscles. It is as one approaches old age that they most seem comfortable with clothing that just feels good and draws no attention to them.

In prison, inmates must wear the same clothing so as not to be set apart in any way from others, creating envy, strife or disorder.

Yet God looks on the inner person, the clothing that comes from faith in Jesus Christ. He looks into the heart, and sees individuals — and He loves them. Paul wrote of this kind of clothing in Galatians 5:22-23: "But the fruit of the Spirit is love, joy, peace, longsuffering, kindness, goodness, faithfulness, gentleness, self-control. Against such there is no law."

What do you wear? Do you worry about external clothing that changes over time, and that is subject to trends and fashions? This kind lends evidence that you are tossed about by the will of other men and women and will always leave you unsatisfied. If you sit in prison, do you hate the sameness of your uniform that just makes you a number?

Or do you wear the internal character evidenced by the fruit of the Spirit? These are the clothes that really make the man, and bear fruit that lasts for eternity.

Letter Ten:
A Rock at Rock Bottom

Genesis 49:24

"Joseph's bow remained steady, his strong arms stayed limber because of the Shepherd, the Rock of Israel."

Ken,

"Bustin' Rocks!" That's the classic task of prisoners sentenced to hard labor. It is a little more sophisticated now than breaking rocks. But emotionally, prison is still difficult.

Ken, a man is divested of his freedom, and faces depression and cynicism in prison. I don't bust rocks, but I have sometimes hit rock bottom emotionally and spiritually. And I wonder how Joseph made it through his ordeal.

Possibly the key to Joseph's endurance while in prison is in Jacob's blessing recorded in Genesis 49. One of Jacob's longest blessings to his 12 sons went to Joseph. Although the blessing has to do with the future of the tribe of Joseph, it reflects upon Joseph's very own character. The blessing says, "Joseph's bow remained steady, his strong arms stayed limber."

Steady and limber lived Joseph throughout the extreme ups and downs of his life. He went from favorite son to slave to top man in Potiphar's household to prison to second in command of all Egypt. Unstable and difficult circumstances called for a steady and limber response from Joseph. I guess that is one reason I admire Joseph so much.

How could Joseph stay so steady after the heartbreak of being sold into slavery to a distant country by his very own brothers? How could Joseph stay limber having been unjustly convicted and relegated to a life of atrophy in prison? The power that kept Joseph's bow steady and arms limber is described clearly in the blessing of Jacob upon Joseph. "…because of the Shepherd, the Rock of Israel." When Joseph hit rock bottom the Rock of Israel kept him steady.

In my many years of prison confinement, I have hit rock bottom emotionally a few times, Ken. And it was traumatic. But I found that instead of life here being between a rock and a hard place, life here is a matter of the Rock being between me and a hard place.

The same solid Rock of Israel has kept me steady that kept Joseph. When far beyond my own abilities to sustain myself in a stable form, The Shepherd, the Rock of Israel, Jesus Christ, gave me firmness. With Joseph in mind, I sing, "On Christ the solid rock I stand, all other ground is sinking sand."

Ken, may the Lord, the Rock, keep your bow steady and arms limber.

On the Rock,

Tom

◆ ◆ ◆

Tom,

For many of us the scenes of "bustin rock" are vivid and cherished memories of moral movies made, unlike what we often see today. We always seemed to be rooting for the good guy no matter what the crime might be. I guess nothing has changed.

Hollywood would often show the protagonist hitting rock bottom, but their salvation came when they literally busted out of prison. They never did present the Rock of Ages as their real salvation and way out of prison. I suppose this is to be expected.

Tom, as I look at your life I think of 1 Corinthians 10:4, the passage on which the great hymn "Rock of Ages" was based. Paul writes, "and all drank the same spiritual drink, for they were drinking from a spiritual rock which, followed them; and the rock was Christ."

The God who led Israel out of "prison of Egypt," who appeared to them in the pillar of cloud by day and of fire by night, who gave them His Law and brought them into the promised land, was Christ. The same Christ who died for us on the cross and arose in glory.

The people of the Old and the New Testaments are one people; they are all under Christ. For this reason, He gave them similar blessings: first circumcision — a type of baptism; first a type of spiritual eating and drinking, then the sacrament of eating and drinking His true body and blood in the Lord's Supper. Behind that manna and that water in the desert were the power and the presence of Christ just as He was in the pillar at the sea and in the dry road through the sea. Never once did he leave his people.

Tom, we are drinking from that same rock as the children of Israel did when Moses led them through the wilderness so many years ago. And as they were freed from slavery and Egyptian pursuit, and led into the promised land, so we too are freed from the oppression of sin, death and the devil to our eternal promised land in heaven. There we shall commune with the Rock of Israel — even Jesus Christ.

I love verse three of the hymn "Rock of Ages" the most, as it gives me the greatest comfort:

> Nothing in my hand I bring,
> Simply to thy cross I cling;
> Naked, come to Thee for dress;
> Helpless, look to Thee for grace;
> Foul, I to the fountain fly-
> Wash me, Savior, or I die!

In Christ,

Ken

When things turn rocky

Someone has suggested that those times in life when everything seems in order and life runs smoothly are only momentary respites from real life. Real life is a series of intermingled stresses, disappointments and trials. From a human standpoint, we are more often caught between a rock and a hard place in a valley, than standing free on a mountain top.

Yet, depending upon which foundation we build our lives, we can still be people of joy. Jesus spoke of the house built on sand, washed away by the storms of life. He offers the house built on a Rock, against which nothing life can offer will prevail.

A human life — our earthly house — built on a Rock stands comfortably during days of light breezes and moderate temperatures; unmovable against the most fierce storms of nature. It offers warmth during the cool of night, and perfect cooling during the fierce heat of high noon.

Standing on this Rock, that is, building a life on the foundation of faith in Jesus Christ, places the "Rock being between me and a hard place."

Peter writes in I Peter 2:6-7, "Therefore it is also contained in the Scripture, 'Behold, I lay in Zion a chief cornerstone, elect, precious, and he who believes on Him will by no means be put to shame.' Therefore, to you who believe, He is precious; but to those who are disobedient, 'The stone which the builders rejected has become the chief cornerstone'..."

Jesus is the foundational Rock. He is the Cornerstone, and the Capstone. In Christ, you are set free from being between the rocks.

Are you still living in bondage to shifting sands, hopelessly victimized by all of life's trials? Or do you have the peace of God that passes all understanding, the peace that comes from resting on the Rock, even Jesus Christ?

Letter Eleven:
Father Figuring (June 2000)

Genesis 37:33-34

"...'Joseph has surely been torn to pieces.' Then Jacob tore his clothes, put on sackcloth and mourned for his son many days."

Ken,

Father's Day is coming up soon. It is a difficult time.
It is hard to figure how I could be a father figure to my children. I only see my three children twice a year and my own father, at four-score years, is quite limited in his travels.
While dwelling on how much I have missed of my children's lives, a hollow sadness overtakes me. But then I talk with a man (I'll call him Jake) who after 15 years is getting out of prison soon.
Jake explained to me that his previous wife, so deeply angered and appalled at his crime, decided to tell her two-year old that his dad died in a car accident. This son, now 16, has believed all of his youth that his dad was dead. Maybe some people would say, "Serves him right! Commit a crime; pay the penalty!" But, Ken does a lie to a son serve anyone right?
This Father's Day my thoughts turn again to the story of Joseph and Jacob as a father figure. Jacob thought Joseph was dead due to the deceit of his other sons. Jacob could not be comforted (v. 35) in his long, hard mourning process. For years the deceit continued. Jacob could not pray for Joseph, could not visit Joseph, nor could he write to him or mount a rescue for him. Jacob knew Joseph to be

dead, devoured by a wild beast. Little did Jacob know that Joseph's existence had been devoured by the lying mouths of his brothers.

It was ironic, divine justice that the lying tongues that brought the "news" of Joseph's death to Jacob, years later would bring these truthful tidings to Jacob, "Joseph is still alive! In fact, he is ruler of all of Egypt!"

Ken, can you imagine the anger and confusion running through Jacob's mind at that moment? But cast all those matters aside; the most important fact stood out — Joseph was alive. "The spirit of their father Jacob revived." (Genesis 45)

I can't help but realize how blessed I am that my children love, support and believe me. I am proud of them and they respect me as their father.

The greatness of my own father's love, like Jacob's, is hard for me to figure out or fathom. He prays for me, visits me, seeks my release.

Ken, for all the days I have been in prison, dad has written me every day.

I cannot tell you how far the love of my father has carried me through these trying years. Please join me in praying for his well-being while awaiting my release.

We know the over-arching historical significance of Jacob's clan joining Joseph in Egypt; but on a personal level, the image of Father Jacob and Son Joseph reuniting after so many years and tears gives me hope.

Father figuring is not a matter of counting days and years, it is heart, character and Christ-like love.

Blessed Father's Day,

Tom

(Rev. Ralph Bird died on May 9, 2002 and was buried next to his wife Virginia Bird in Hardy, Arkansas. Tom was not allowed to attend either funeral.)

◆ ◆ ◆

Tom,

Your thoughts on "Father Figuring" remind me of my own father who has been with the Lord since 1982. I sometimes wonder how long that is in the eternity of heaven — or nestled in the bosom of Abraham as Jesus told the story. In any case, we watch time as it passes by, but for my father, time is no longer a concern, just a wonderful and endless bliss of forever.

Thoughts of teaching confirmation class also come to mind. Do you remember when our fathers taught us about our heavenly Father from Luther's Small Catechism? I think about this from time to time. Question # 105 asks, "Why do you here call the First Person of the Trinity 'the Father?' " The answer: "I call Him the Father because He is the Father of my Lord Jesus Christ and also my Father." In one of the proof texts Jesus said, "I ascend unto My Father and your Father, and to My God and your God." (John 20:17)

Isn't it amazing that we have the same Father, God Himself? You in a Kansas prison and me in a Minnesota pulpit? He is our Father because He created us and because He redeemed us in His Son.

The whole world of people are biological brothers and sisters because of their common heritage as descendants of Adam and Eve. But this family relationship is even more significant and precious to us because we have been made spiritual brothers and sisters through Christ's death and resurrection. Faith in Christ's entire work finished on Calvary makes us so. This also encourages us to reconnect to our world family with the Gospel.

Oh, how important it is that His message of forgiveness goes forth. I proclaim the Gospel here in Burnsville and you proclaim it in Lansing.

Tom, as Jacob missed Joseph, thinking him dead, still continuing to live on in life through grace, so too is your father. Rev. Ralph Bird misses you, his beloved son. He knows that you are physically and spiritually alive in Lansing and serving Christ. And at the same time, you as a father are missing your beloved children (Andrea, Paul, Aaron), yet you know where each other are and remain confident of each other's love. This is a tearful and painful blessing. Someday you will all be together. And our heavenly Father knows when that time will be, though he feels your heartache now.

Your dad has told me many times of what an obedient son you were. And your children, although being with you for such a short time, were very much guided by your fatherly instruction and example.

The great reward that we have as our possession is not only the love of God in Christ but also the love of our children, and you also have the love of hundreds of other fellow believers who pray for you. God has exercised you, His "saint," in a different way since you stepped into prison in 1984. And His "saint" has shown his trust in Christ and has sought His will through it all. As Christ said, "blessed are those..." Tom, I am rejoicing with you because we, and all believers in Christ, are a part of the "those."

Happy Heavenly Father's Day,

Ken

◆ ◆ ◆

First commandment with a promise

"Honor your father and your mother, that your days may be long upon the land which the LORD your God is giving you." (Exodus 20:12)

How obvious it is that we were born of earthly parents. Our existence and biology proves this. Yet many bring dishonor on their parents; through rebellion, disassociation, abandonment, and some, through a life of crime. Some earthly parents, too, have done the same to their children and have lost their position of honor.

Many humans sit in manmade prisons of brick and mortar. Others sit in manmade prisons of spiritual rebellion, and this is a more serious issue than the former.

In God our Heavenly Father, we have one who loves us unconditionally, who will never fail us, whose Spirit pleads with us to submit to His love. God gave up His most precious possession to re-establish His Fatherhood with us. This happened when Jesus, the Son of God, gave His own life on a cross, and God raised Him from the dead three days later. Now Jesus lives with His Father in Heaven, and is our advocate.

As we are to honor our earthly parents, so, too, should we honor our Heavenly Father, and in so honoring Him by trusting His Son with our lives, He adopts us as His children. As His adopted child, we gain eternity with Him and the goodness of His Kingdom.

Do you honor your earthly parents? If you honor God by trusting His Son, you will honor your Heavenly Father, and He will give you the strength and insight to honor your parents. That is His promise.

It is the key to a true, happy Father's Day.

Letter Twelve:
When Milestones Become Millstones

Genesis 39:2

"And the Lord was with Joseph, so he became a successful man. And he was in the house of his master the Egyptian."

Ken,

Did you know that Job was such a genius that he spoke on the very first day of his birth? The Bible is true and it says it. Job 3:1, "...Job opened his mouth and cursed the day he was born." Bad interpretation! Old Joke! But I am getting kind of old.

It is no joking matter that I have passed age 50 now. It was not an easy transition to move past that milestone.

Seriously, Ken, have you ever, like Job, cursed the day you were born? I did. Like many holidays and special days like birthdays and anniversaries, I get depressed. The day before my 50th birthday, I cursed the day I was born. Besides having a terrible day, the realization that so much of my life is wasted and I have been unable to be neither a father to my children nor a husband to my wife gets to me.

What does a person do when life's milestones become millstones around their neck?

I turn to my Bible mentor, Joseph. Amidst the up and down life of Joseph there is one steady, consistent, sure pattern. In slavery, "The Lord was with Joseph" (Genesis 39:2). In prison, "The Lord was with Joseph." (Genesis 39:21) When he stood before Pharaoh and Joseph's freedom depended on his interpretation of Pharaoh's dreams, Joseph said, "I cannot do it but God will give Pharaoh the answer he desires." (Genesis 41:16)

When Joseph's two sons were born, he made known his awareness of the Lord's presence in his life. He named his firstborn son, Manasseh and said, "It is because God has made me forget my trouble and all my father's household." The second son he named Ephraim and said, "It is because God has made me fruitful in the land of my suffering." (Genesis 41:51-52)

The Lord was with Joseph to draw him out of his misery and depression.

Ken, of the many aspects of our worship service that we quickly take for granted is the salutation from the worship leader: "The Lord be with thee," and the response: "And with thy spirit." Oh, how we so often without mind or spirit buzz by these precious words of blessing. The generic and shallow worship services here in prison rarely contain the salutation, "The Lord be with thee." I miss that tremendously now.

Joseph was alone, yet held to his faith in the Lord's presence. We have a great fellowship of believers who should always be assuring one another, "The Lord be with you."

For Joseph in his lonely roller coaster ride of life, the most important, stabilizing fact of faith he held was "the Lord was with him." I repent of my cursing the day of my birth. For to curse my birth is to curse the Lord who created and sustains me. That is sin.

The Lord is truly with me. Milestones are no longer millstones tied around my neck, when I walk in faith and grasp tightly the promise that "The Lord is with me."

And the Lord be with you,

Tom

◆ ◆ ◆

Tom,

I am happy that you still have a sense of humor — it encourages me. To tell you the truth, I have never heard that old joke about Job, so it is not an old joke to me, even though compared to you, I am old.

I have often wondered how Job could curse the day he was born. It seems to me that cursing the day of one's birth is a risky thing. I imagine God striking me dead should I say such a thing. But Job said it and God let him live, so there must have been a purpose in recording it for us to read and contemplate.

It is my feeling that Christians who suffer unjustly have a unique understanding of the suffering of Job. Through suffering, the Holy Spirit gives them insights about the human condition, both to comfort themselves and to share Christ's love with others. They are able, then, to press God for His promise of forgiveness and in the end receive a needed blessing. For our Lord says, "to whom much is given much is expected." And, "Blessed is he whose transgression is forgiven." (Romans 4:7)

And, lest we forget Job did prosper in the end.

But to your question as to what a person can do when life's milestones become millstones: I think you answered it. It is the answer I give to my parishioners, especially when they feel broken and oppressed. It is the answer that I, too, hopefully would receive should I find myself in such agonizing human hurt.

I wonder if suffering does not also drive us to better appreciate what is included in God's eternal will! Luther asks that very question (LSC.156): "What does the good and gracious will of God include?" Among things God does for us and we do and avoid for Him, it also includes "everything that God wants us to suffer patiently according to His good pleasure."

When the Apostle Paul was nearly stoned to death in Lystra he told many of the disciples that, "we must through much tribulation enter into the Kingdom of God." (Acts 14:22) And Jesus said, "If any man will come after Me, let him deny himself and take up his cross and follow Me." (Matthew 16:24)

Tom, this is all very easy for me to say since I have not suffered like Paul or like yourself. Still, the words of Jesus are true whether or not all Christians have experienced equally the same kind of hurt.

It is so true that Joseph experienced a roller-coaster kind of life — the favorite son and the hated brother, the slave and Potiphar's trusted servant, the prisoner and second in command to the great Pharaoh — all of this as a result of God's providence and mercy. And it is equally true that "the Lord was with Joseph." (Genesis 39:2)

Tom, we know by faith that our caring Christ is with us always. Still, it seems so unfair that some who are guilty are granted liberty or never brought to justice, while others endure imprisonment that they do not deserve. But in the end, we will live in eternal freedom because of Christ's sacrificial suffering on the cross. He does forgive us of our sins — and not just our sins but the sins of the whole world.

When we bask in Christ's work of redemption, we know that by God-given faith He has made us one with Him and at peace with God and men. Yes, we are one with Christ because He is at peace with us. He is also in us. Nothing brings me more comfort and rest than that.

Tom, I confess that when you speak of some of the wonderful aspects of the pastoral ministry, like pronouncing the salutation in the worship service, I am reminded of my failure to pay attention to it. Sometimes when I speak the blessing, "The Lord be with you," my mind passes over the return blessing of the congregation, "And with thy spirit." I think the devil is happy with my sinful lapse of memory.

Yes, many Sundays go by when I drift and turn from this simple but profound blessing of the Lord. It is a sin that I have to repent of often because I commit it so often. But through Jesus' death on the cross, such sins have been forgiven! As Paul reminds us, "Christ also has loved us and given Himself for us, an offering and a sacrifice to God..." (Ephesians 5:2) And the sweetest words in Scripture for us are: "There is therefore now no condemnation to those who are in Christ Jesus." (Romans 8:1)

Tom, thank you for reminding me of what is so precious to all of us.

The Lord is with us, my brother.

Ken

♦ ♦ ♦

But is the Lord with you?

"The LORD bless you and keep you; the LORD make His face shine upon you, and be gracious to you; the LORD lift up His countenance upon you, and give you peace." (Numbers 6:24-26)

Moses spoke these words to his brother Aaron, Israel's high priest. He wanted Aaron to know that God was with him no matter where his journey took him, in good times and bad, whether in wanderings and or when settled.

Aaron made a terrible mistake during the same time that Moses met God on Mount Sinai. While Moses received the Ten Commandments from God, Aaron allowed the Israelites to worship a golden calf, a serious abomination toward God. God could have struck Aaron dead.

Instead, God forgave Aaron, and the man learned from his mistakes. He moved forward and left the old ways behind, and became the revered father of a priestly lineage.

God walked with Aaron because by faith, Aaron repented and walked with God. "The just shall live by faith," wrote the prophet Habakkuk.

People of faith know this, that no matter their circumstances, the Lord is with them. Is the Lord with you? Are you a person of faith?

Can you say with the writer of Hebrews, "Now may the God of peace who brought up our Lord Jesus from the dead, that great Shepherd of the sheep, through the blood of the everlasting covenant, make you complete in every good work to do His will, working in you what is well pleasing in His sight, through Jesus Christ, to whom be glory forever and ever. Amen." Hebrews 13:20-21

The Lord be with you.

Letter Thirteen:
On Wheat, Weeds & Waiting

Genesis 37:18-20

"When they saw him from a distance and before he came close to them, they plotted against him to put him to death. And they said to one another, Here comes this dreamer! Now then, come and let us kill him and throw him into one of the pits; and we will say, 'A wild beast devoured him.' Then let us see what will become of his dreams!"

Ken,

Joseph's brother thought it was wrong that Joseph snitched on them, that Joseph was their dad's favorite, that Joseph thought himself superior, that Joseph dreamed dreams that demeaned them. So these self-righteous fellows became judge, jury and almost executioners.

Acts of self-righteousness are a major problem in our world and churches today as it has always been. It is an enemy of God's grace. Joseph's brothers did it, the Pharisees did it and even Jesus' disciples did it. Jesus, in Matthew 13:24-29, 36-43, gives a strong warning about the self-righteous business of separating weeds and wheat in the world.

We see evil like weeds growing up and we hate it. We want to do something about it. Like the servants in the parable of the weeds and the wheat, we say to the owner of the world, "Do you want us to go and pull them up?" The answer from God the owner is a definite, "NO!"

In our world, we need the judicial system. Otherwise, anarchy and revenge would prevail. But sometimes in the awesome challenge of judicial work, the system fails or people in the system fail. Sometimes it fails to convict the guilty; sometimes it fails to acquit the innocent. So here at Lansing Correctional Facility, there are many weeds and some wheat that has been pulled elsewhere and replanted here.

Some of my brothers in the ministry have shared with me the unsettling conclusion that, "Tom, only the Lord knows what happened that night." In this 21st Century, we are used to all mysteries being brought to a conclusion within 60 minutes interrupted by an occasional commercial interlude. We find it hard to say, "We don't know what happened or who is guilty." Somebody has got to be weeded out or we will never find "closure." "Closure;" is that not a much over used word today?

Ken, there is a weed in Emporia, Kansas. He is a false witness, that you had the privilege of looking in the eye at a bookstore promotion of *Caged Bird*. Over the years, I have wanted him to be weeded out. But some things have to wait.

Jesus said, "No. Because, while pulling the weeds, you may root up the wheat with the them." (Matthew 13:29) I don't know the hearts of the false witnesses, the investigators, the gossips, the prosecutors, the jurors, the reporters in my case, just as they do not know my heart. The truth is we are all sinful beings falling short of God's glory.

What I do know is that at the harvest, "The Son of Man will send out His angels, and they will weed out of His Kingdom everything that causes sin." (Matthew 13:41)

Joseph's brothers could not wait; they sought to weed Joseph out. They did not know that Joseph was wheat to be plucked out and replanted in Egypt for a high purpose. Their act that sought to destroy God's prophetic plan actually fulfilled it.

Ken, I can't sort it all out; that's the angel's job in the end.

Meanwhile, we plant and till.

In Peace,

Tom

◆ ◆ ◆

Tom,

    This may be as good a place as any to take issue with another baffling question: how the sons of Jacob and the direct descendants of Abraham could ever have become so sullied and stoop so low as to plan the murder of a blood brother and then sell him into slavery?

    I saw this at first as a family squabble, like dealing with an injustice in the church. But, I also see it applying to the state. Abraham's law would certainly have been passed down from him and should have guided their lives, but their actions showed they were indifferent to it.

    The character of Joseph's brothers may very well be the result of a broken home — a home lacking unity and true discipline. Jacob's polygamy, I'm sure, helped to produce rebellious children. And the brothers neglected to watch and pray, and so fell victim to their sinful desires. They acted as judge, jury, and, almost, executioner. See what they did.

    They watched Joseph in secrecy from a distance. They saw that their father looked kindly upon Joseph and when he made Joseph a coat of many colors, they deeply resented it. Their intent is clear in the words, "they plotted against him."

    First they mocked: "Look, here comes this dreamer." So, they judged him as a "dreamer" and in doing so mocked the Lord's chosen one.

    Their plan took shape quickly: to slay him and cast his body into a pit, then cover up the murder with a lie. And they said it without any feeling, making their intent to be cold-blooded murderers.

    The 10 remaining sons of Jacob were his legal heirs by blood, but they abused their office of sonship in what they did. I relate their actions to our modern judicial system — to those who each have a part of the legal obligation to serve as judge, jury and executioner of a sentence. They hold this office by legal right, but they abuse it when they stubbornly ignore truth and search for gossip to get a conviction, destroying the life of an innocent son. I see these participants in the same way as the brothers of Joseph.

The story, though, does not stop with Joseph in the pit, as the brothers sold him into slavery. Then came Joseph's incarceration, and after some time, God set Joseph up as second in command to Pharaoh. Later, when Joseph confronted his brothers during the famine, he set them at ease and showed great wisdom when he said, "You meant evil against me, but God meant it for good in order to bring about this present result to preserve many people alive." (Gen. 0:20)

Tom, just as the injustice perpetrated against Joseph by his brothers brought glory to God and saved the lives of "many people," so the injustice that fell upon you by citizen brothers will, in the end, redound to the glory of God, to the benefit of society and to your own spiritual good. I believe that you will be vindicated, as was Joseph.

As for the weed in Emporia, that witness who testified against you, he surely did frighten me that day we met face-to-face. I saw seething anger and hatred in his eyes. He reminded me of the proverb, "The wicked flee when no one pursues him."

Still, we believe that the good work of justice must eventually be done since the initial keeping of the law flows from faith. We are accounted righteous before God for Christ's sake by faith. I continue to pray the Emporian accuser will come to believe that we have a gracious God who knows all things, who demands repentance and who forgives all of our sins because of Christ's sacrificial death on the cross.

That is the message of hope I see in Genesis 37. It may be covered in mystery, but it's there nonetheless in the last sentence of verse 19, "Then let us see what will become of his dreams!" Whether Joseph's brothers knew it or not, ironically they whispered a word of prophesy. They judged his dreams as grandiose and him as arrogant, but little did they know that what they mocked was of

God and would happen. In a wonderful way, the brothers became the beneficiaries of Joseph's ascent to power, which he attributed to the grace and mercy of God.

Tom, I am thankful that God has chosen and fitted you to perform a task so precious and pleasing to him. You have taken to Lansing Prison's "Egypt" the saving gospel of Jesus Christ; that those in your hearing should learn that God no longer charges their sins to them, but declares them righteous in Christ.

Blessings my brother,

Ken

♦ ♦ ♦

And they thought they had planted weeds

Paul wrote in Romans 8:28, "And we know that all things work together for good to those who love God, to those who are the called according to His purpose."

Circumstances often overwhelm us, and when we are the cause of our bad situation, we may wish that someone, even God, would just pluck us out and throw us in a fire. At least we would be done with suffering.

Overwhelming circumstances are made even worse when we are innocent of their cause. We wish to lash out at those who have harmed us and bring to them the same or worse punishment than that which we received. They gloat, and we growl.

But wait!

God has planted you right where you are to serve His purpose, a higher calling, and it is a calling you could never realize were it not for your circumstances. More so, you may never know the results of your planting until you have begun a new life in eternity.

For those who love God, circumstances do not have to hinder usefulness or destroy their mission. If you love God, look for His mission where you are, not where you want to be, for in all things,

God can work for good for His glory and to your benefit.
Those who gloat will continue to do so, while you grow and enjoy God's abundant life, right in the middle of your circumstances.

Letter Fourteen:
On Setting Records Straight

Genesis 41:14

"Then Pharaoh sent and called for Joseph, and they hurriedly brought him out of the prison; and when he had shaved himself and changed his clothes, he came to Pharaoh."

Ken,

To be falsely accused and convicted is heart wrenching. I have shared with my wife Terry, with other family members and with close friend like you that I cannot rest or go to my grave until the record is set straight. Exoneration! I have been obsessed with that goal.

My wife has reminded me that such an obsession itself could be a prison and that it might tear me up and tear us apart. Such an obsession could take away all the rich blessings we do have for the rest of our lives. But I am stubborn and I am not always a good listener in spite of the wisdom of my wife. After all, how can I leave prison with my head held high unless fully exonerated? How can I reenter the ordained ministry unless I can present before the certification board the official record declaring my innocence?

In the midst of this turmoil, I must humble myself before Scripture and in particular the story of Joseph in prison in Egypt. I asked myself, "Was Joseph ever exonerated of rape?"

If a renowned archeologist would dig up the preserved archives of the legal documents of ancient Egypt, he might very well find that Joseph remains "on the record" as a felony rapist. The Biblical record is silent in regard to Joseph and the issue of exoneration. The Scripture simply says, "So Pharaoh sent for Joseph." Pharaoh needed him, found him useful and called upon him. Nothing more is said. The exoneration issue became a non-issue. Pharaoh, and God through this Pharaoh, used Joseph.

It seems the lesson is that a person's usefulness far outweighs a person's past record.

Look at Martin Luther, once denounced as an outlaw with a price on his head. He was never exonerated officially. Yet was he not considered as one of the top ten most influential people in the history of the last millennium?

When my life is over, I really would like the record to have been set straight. But more importantly, in my final years, in some small proportion to Joseph, I would like to be called from this prison to contribute something to society and church by the grace of our Lord and to His glory.

Your friend in Christ,

Tom

◆ ◆ ◆

Tom,

When I first read your letter my mind became distracted; I suddenly realized how lightly I have treated the significance of God's command to have a good reputation and be worthy of respect. Yet, in I Timothy 3:7a, Paul wrote of spiritual leaders, "Moreover he must have a good report of them which are without." And in Eccl 7:1a, Solomon wrote, "A good name is better than precious ointment."

When a person enjoys a good name he often takes it for granted. Yet if circumstances conspire to steal a good man's name, it is then he begins to yearn to clear himself, and he sees more clearly how precious it is to be worthy of respect. As we go about our business here on the outside of prison, we tend to forget how important this is. You, however, know in a deeply painful manner what the loss of a good name and reputation means.

You say, "I cannot rest or go to my grave until the record is set straight. Exoneration! I have been obsessed with that goal." I think you are too harsh with yourself when you make that charge against yourself.

I found a good definition of exoneration. It comes from two Latin words: *ex* meaning "off," and *onus* meaning "burden." It means, "to free from a burden; to free from blame; to release from a responsibility or obligation." This is our goal and it is a powerful and proper motivator. I think it is passion for righteousness that drives you, not obsession.

Potiphar's wife falsely accused Joseph of raping her, and her accusation placed an innocent man in prison. It destroyed his good name and reputation.

Pharaoh, though, had an urgent need. He cared little about who would interpret his dream, but he was obsessed with unlocking its secrets. He summoned Joseph because of the report that he could interpret dreams. Joseph's past made no difference to him. The text is silent about whether anyone reminded Pharaoh that Joseph was a felony rapist. In any case, it did not matter. What mattered was that Pharaoh set Joseph free from prison. And this is very important when compared to your case: Joseph's reputation in prison was exemplary. Once out of prison, his actions enhanced his reputation and he gained a powerful name, one that generated respect from the Egyptians and other nations.

In the Eighth Commandment, Luther explained how important this: "Besides our own body, or wife or husband, and our temporal property, we have one more treasure which is indispensable to us, namely, our honor and good name, for it is intolerable to live among men in public disgrace and contempt. Therefore God will not have our neighbor deprived of his reputation, honor, and character any more than of his money and possessions; he would have every man maintain his self-respect before his wife, children, servants, and neighbors. In its first and simplest meaning, this commandment pertains to public courts of justice, where a poor, innocent man is accused and maligned by false witnesses and consequently punished in his body, property, or honor." (*Book of Concord*, Tap., 399.254ff).

Tom, I believe that we have an obligation to our family, friends, and most of all to God Himself to set the record straight and clear our good name.

In the Kingdom of God, believers in Jesus have already been exonerated and they desire this for others. This happened when Christ paid for all the sins of mankind on the cross and when we by faith accept it. Forgiveness does not flow from arrogant pride-filled hearts, but from hearts smitten by the tragedy of their sins and attracted by the beauty of the Gospel. We have all felt this.

Tom, you and I both know what it is like for God to forgive us. May this move us to forgive those who have sinned against us.
Still, as Luther and Scripture confirms, God places great value on public exoneration as well. So your honorable and righteous struggle continues. And I, along with hundreds of others, stand with you.

I believe that some day I will welcome you to freedom outside the gates; that will only compound the joy you now have of freedom in your heart. And then we will work together, along with the others, to create an atmosphere where you can contribute even more to society and to the church, where God's grace in Christ is more visibly seen.

Remember that God's greatest works through Joseph came after his release from prison.

Blessings, my brother Joseph,

Ken

◆ ◆ ◆

Your name can be cleared

Prisons burst at the seams with men and women who have been caught doing evil acts to obtain gold or power or sensual pleasure. It is impossible to know how many others, who have done the same things yet, who have never been caught, still live free.

An even greater number of people have not committed felony crimes but *have* made pursuit of worldly treasures the center of their lives, and by doing so, have tarnished their good name. Which of us does not know at least a few of them? They have disregarded their family, worry nothing about offending neighbors, or offend all of society with their trash talk or public displays of repulsive behavior.

Many who *have* been convicted, some by juries and more by the Holy Spirit working through their conscience, have become distraught at their own degradation, embarrassed and even depressed.

"And I saw the dead, small and great, standing before God, and books were opened. And another book was opened, which is the Book of Life. And the dead were judged according to their works, by the things which were written in the books. The sea gave up the dead who were in it, and Death and Hades delivered up the dead who were in them. And they were judged, each one according to his works. Then Death and Hades were cast into the lake of fire. This is the second death. And anyone not found written in the Book of Life was cast into the lake of fire." (Revelation 20:12-15)

The names in the Lamb's book of life have all received exoneration from the Only One Who can offer it, even God through Jesus Christ. By faith in Jesus Christ, your name, too, can be cleared for all eternity.

Those who have received Jesus Christ have found a new life, a new name — Christian — and have been exonerated. And though mankind may still call them "felon," the One Who truly matters calls them "forgiven."

Do you need to clear your name? Do you seek forgiveness? Or exoneration? God in Christ Jesus has already given it to all who, by faith, believe on His name. Even you.

Letter Fifteen:
Unique Not Special

Genesis 37:2

"Now Israel loved Joseph more than any of his other sons…"

Ken,

Often, the young inner city children of Grace Lutheran School grasp the skirt or cling to the arms of my wife Terry, the Principal. Their love-starved eyes gaze up to her as if to say, "I want to be special." Now Terry loves these children and to her each is unique; but she must ever be mindful of treating someone "special."

We all grew up experiencing anger and jealousy toward the dreaded "teacher's pet." So Terry loves each child uniquely; but not specially to the exclusion of others.

Now Joseph was treated by his father Israel, both uniquely and specially to the exclusion of the rest of the brothers. That's what got this whole saga of Joseph started. Joseph milked all he could out of the special treatment by his father. In Genesis 37:1 it says, "Joseph…brought their father a bad report about them [the brothers]." Joseph was a teacher's pet and a snitch.

Recently, I became eligible for parole for the first time. The parole board was to evaluate whether I was "suitable" for parole release. Now there is no doubt in anyone's mind that my record in prison for 16 years is outstanding nor is there any doubt that I will be a law-abiding productive citizen on the outside. So I am suitable.

But the parole board approaches their job as appointees of the governor of the people for the state of Kansas. Nowadays, the people demand a get-tough policy on those convicted and they demand a weighty voice to victim's rights. So the parole board chose to approach me uniquely, but not specially.

They were presented an overwhelmingly positive show of support from wife, children, relatives, friends, past, present and future associates and even a great book about my life. All of this was the likes of which they had never seen before. But from their perspective, the people demand more time of convicted felons.

I was not specially treated. With the fell swoop of a pen I was given four more years to serve. It is not right; but from their perspective, it was fair because everyone in my situation must do at least 20 years. In their view, it is not their job to determine guilt or innocence; that's the court's job. It's a painful contradiction. They don't know the truth, so what they did was fair, but not right.

So I run and cling to the arms of the Lord and ask Him to please treat me as special. Christ's answer is, "I love you and My blood was given and shed for you; but I will not treat you special to the exclusion of others."

Christ is not Israel who gives special gifts to his "favorites." But the Lord does have a unique plan for each of His children.

To put it into perspective, the same day I was devastated by the parole board's decision to keep me in prison at least four more years, 13,000 or more people were killed in a catastrophic earthquake in India. I cannot imagine the pain of the families at that kind of loss. My loss pales in comparison to them, and I am no more special or valuable than these people.

Am I to be angry at God because of my continual loss of freedom? He loves me and has a unique plan for me. Being Israel's special son left Joseph in a pit; being God's uniquely planned child, Joseph was sent ahead to Egypt to save his people.

Your unique friend,

Tom

◆ ◆ ◆

Tom,

    We know by nature that showing favoritism is wrong as it will most likely result in jealousy and hatred. Yet Biblical patriarchs did it all the time, and we remain uncritical of their behavior. Perhaps we feel that since God chose them for His "special" purpose, whatever they did is excusable in the light of the bigger story. I don't think God excuses this behavior in me nor do I think He excuses it in the patriarchs. Terry, your wife, instinctively knows and experiences this. Perhaps we should emphasize this more to our Sunday School children.

    In Genesis 37, Moses speaks of this favoritism without comment, as if he believed we would know it is wrong. "Now Israel loved Joseph more than any of his other sons...And his brothers saw that their father loved him more than all his brothers; and so they hated him and could not speak to him on friendly terms." (Genesis 37:3,4)

    This statement, made without censure, describes an event that had imponderable and nearly tragic results. It brought a great deal of strife to the family. I wonder if we parents realize that when we show love for one child and not the other we might plant in them the seed that would lead to a terrible injustice? Yet it happened to Jacobs' family.

    I am sure it is common that children born to aging parents do enjoy preference and, in some ways, become like pets. In Jacob's case, other factors contributed to make his preference more pronounced.

    The outward distinction that Jacob bestowed on Joseph was "a long-sleeved coat." Luther suggested that Jacob saw Joseph as a ruler and indicated this by making the coat of many and bright colors. This garment was, then, suited to a prince or a king, not a shepherd boy. By this gift, Jacob visually told his other sons that he thought Joseph should enjoy preeminence over them.

    Joseph's dreams created additional hostility.

    It got to the point where the brothers were no longer "able to speak peaceably with him." This created an insurmountable problem for Joseph, much like your own problem. Even though Joseph was a "snitch" as you put it, and sinful, God used his difficult situation for his unique good and sealed Israel's future. All believers in Christ benefited. In like manner, you and other believers can still benefit from the injustice you have experienced, even that which resulted from the negative decision of the 2000 parole board.

I can appreciate the legal and moral predicament of the parole board. They must adhere to Kansas' law. During their fall 2000 deliberations, the board could not retry your case, nor receive exculpatory evidence that would exonerate you in court, but had only to determine your suitability for parole. Even your proven suitability had an added requirement; that you serve at minimum, 20 years. The decision against parole may have been pre-determined, and unaffected by your exemplary life, work in prison and suitability. You faced a "Catch-22."

Still, we see that our Lord even now is working this out for His greater purpose. I am gratified to know that your life in prison, recognized by all, was done not to merit parole, but because God commanded it of you. In order to exercise your faith in Christ, you did these things willingly. And in this way, Tom, you rendered thanks to our gracious Lord. Your good works, however, are meritorious, but not for the forgiveness of sins (for we obtain this only by faith in Christ) but for other physical and spiritual rewards in this present life and in the life to come. As Paul wrote, "Each shall receive his wages according to his labor." (1 Cor. 3:8)

Tom, the forgiveness God gives to you is the same He gives to all believers in Christ. For Christ died for all and when we by faith accept His sacrificial death on Calvary's cross then, we at that very moment, possess this forgiveness as our own. "Since we are justified by faith, we have peace with God through our Lord Jesus Christ. Through Him we have obtained access by faith." (Romans 5:1)

Faith makes us God's sons. Faith obtains this because faith justifies us and faith has a gracious God. Eternal life then is our possession and home since we have been justified, according to

Scripture, "Those whom he justified he also glorified." (Romans 8:30) God makes us unique in the spiritual realm.

Blessings my brother,

Ken

♦ ♦ ♦

No parole, but a full pardon

"What do you think? If a man has a hundred sheep, and one of them goes astray, does he not leave the ninety-nine and go to the mountains to seek the one that is straying? And if he should find it, assuredly, I say to you, he rejoices more over that sheep than over the ninety-nine that did not go astray." (Matthew 18:12-13)

One of the paradoxes of Christian faith is that God, in Christ Jesus, offers the same wonderful salvation and forgiveness of sins to everyone in the family of mankind, but He also looks on each of us as an only child. Paul wrote in Galatians 3:26-28, "For ye are all the children of God by faith in Christ Jesus. For as many of you as have been baptized into Christ have put on Christ. There is neither Jew nor Greek, there is neither bond nor free, there is neither male nor female: for ye are all one in Christ Jesus."

Truly, without treating anyone special, Jesus died for the sins of mankind; but, He also died for my sins, and for yours.

Inside our beings, we cry out for freedom from sin. We present our case before God, insisting that we have been good and desire to live honorably. But too often, we err, seeking parole instead of pardon.

Parolees are not freed from prison; they may live outside the stone walls and barbed wire, but their prison life still remains. It is simply extended to a new location. The inmate cannot live free, doing what he or she pleases. The parole officer still has control over that inmate, and can pull him or her back inside for the slightest infraction. But Jesus Christ offers us a pardon from sin, and a peace that endures. The Good Shepherd seeks out each of His children who have gone astray and frees them forever, pardoned, not paroled. No manmade prison can contain the soul of one whom Christ has pardoned.

In Jesus, we are an equal child in God's family, yet we are special. And for those who have faith in Christ, a full and eternal pardon is issued. So will you, today, seek a pardon from the One Judge Who is able to grant it — from Jesus Christ?

Letter Sixteen:
And Life Goes On

Genesis 38:1

"At that time Judah left his brothers...married...She became pregnant...Judah got a wife for Er, his firstborn...etc, etc."

Ken,

I've read the story of Joseph at least 100 times. Why? Because Joseph is my Old Testament mentor. With every adversity I face, I ask myself, "What would Joseph do?" I read through Joseph's life like a baying hound pursuing a raccoon. But like such a hound chasing a scent who runs into a fence, I'm often irritated by the interference of Genesis chapter 38. It breaks my train of thought, my focus, my pursuit.

Genesis 38 is a strange little chapter. While not doubting the inspiration of the Holy Spirit, I've often wondered, why is this chapter here? There is nothing about Joseph here. So I normally move quickly along to chapter 39 where I pick up the scent of Joseph and I start baying freely seeking the satisfaction of the hunt for a morsel of wisdom from Joseph's life.

But this last time, while retracing the life of Joseph and again running right into Genesis 38, I was struck. It struck me deep and hard. It was there in those first three simple words of the chapter, "At that time..." I realized then, Ken, the lesson I learned from the words "at that time" was that life goes on.

"At that time" that Joseph was working as a slave, framed for rape, thrown into prison in Egypt-yes at that time-life was going on back in the promised land.

I won't lie, I do cry. I cry sometimes when I think how life is going on without me while I am in prison. My little weathered, stained, smudged address book has addresses and phone numbers blotted out and reentered. Scratched out and written over, these names show movement, change. There are marriages, births, divorces and deaths. Lives of people I care for and who care for me, these lives go on-without me.

I'm sure that Joseph paused often, like me, to wonder about the lives that go on in the world outside of prison. Then it strikes me again that chapter 38 is an important chapter even beyond Joseph's epic tale. This nasty soap-opera-like chapter tells of Judah going to a prostitute who turned out to be his widowed daughter-in-law-he got her pregnant-was going to put her to death. But Tamar lives to give birth to twins, the youngest of which (Perez) usurps the birthright of the oldest. What's the importance?

In Matthew 1:1 it is written, "a record of the genealogy of Jesus Christ the son of David." There in verse three it says, "Judah the father of Perez and Zerah, whose mother was Tamar."

Chapter 38 is part of our sinless Savior's story. The genealogy of Jesus includes some pretty nasty sinners. Yet it is an important part of history.

I'm glad that life went on while Joseph was in prison. It was God's plan. And I'm glad that life goes on for many others while I am in prison. This, too, is God's plan.

Your brother in Christ,

Tom

◆ ◆ ◆

"And it came about at that time, that Judah departed from his brothers, and visited a certain Adullamite, whose name was Hirah." (Genesis 38:1)

Tom,

You brought up a point in your last letter that many of us in the ministry often overlook; namely, to interpret specific words and phrases in the context of the text. Remember how our seminary professors emphasized this aspect of interpretation? It sure is helpful, isn't it?

"At that time" is one of those phrases. These three little words so intrigued me that I searched H.C. Leupold's commentary for help.

Here is what Leupold says: "Is there a strict sequence of time between chapters 37 and 38? It seems so. 'At that time' would mean: just after Joseph had been sold into Egypt. We need not assume that only the climax of the event recorded in this chapter took place after the sale of Joseph. For about twenty-two years intervened between the sale of Joseph and the settlement in Egypt (13 years till Joseph's promotion + 7 years of plenty + 2 years of famine). Judah has time to marry, to have a son, to have a second son whom in his eighteenth year he gives to the same wife; and two years remain for the rest of the events of this chapter. Then the items involved fit closely together: Judah departs from his brethren in vexation over the treatment of their brother Joseph and over their hypocrisy in the sight of their father."

How does all this relate to you and me? Only in that it better helps us to appreciate that, despite Joseph's personal predicament, "life goes on." Joseph continued living, as did Judah — and the Lord continued to commune with both of them, one on the inside and the other, on the outside of prison.

Tom, I look at the 22 years that Joseph endured. During this time, he continued to make his gifts available to Potiphar and Pharaoh. Still, he rejoiced in life even though a great part of it was spent separated from his family. His faith and persistence amazes and motivates me.

I can't help but liken Joseph's years of imprisonment to yours. I am amazed that you continue to endure. It rouses me to anger and humility and yet it also motivates me. I wonder how you do it.

I am saddened that you have missed so many precious moments in the life of your family. What many of us on the outside take for granted — weddings, holidays, births and deaths, even worshiping freely — has been denied to you. At the same time, I witness all the wonderful acts you have done and continue to do at Lansing.

Because of the value of your Kingdom work, we see that your time is being used for the glory of God, and we comfort ourselves. I marvel at your faith, and thus my own faith is strengthened. While rejoicing in your works of faith, I too often overlook your suffering. I wonder how you do it!

It is a difficult burden for anyone to bear. I know your loss of liberty is depressing. I wonder how you do it!

Because of your faith in Christ, I view your suffering differently than I might view that of some of your fellow inmates. When I think of Christ, I know that He endured tremendous suffering. He endured all that we endure — even our personal burden — and yet He did not sin. He endured and He conquered suffering for you and me, and for the whole world.

Yet, no man wants to go through your type of suffering so that he might be in a unique position to minister to others. The resolution of this dilemma lies in your last paragraph: "I'm glad that life went on while Joseph was in prison. It was God's plan. And I'm glad that life goes on for many while I am in prison."

You and Terry once told Dave Racer, the man who chronicled your story in *Caged Bird*, that God's plan for you two includes this time of incarceration. It is not what you want, but it is what you accept. And as long as God wants to use you there, you will continue to serve Him in that place.

Still, I marvel at the life that "goes on" in you through Christ; and I marvel at the life that "goes on" in your suffering. It inspires me to likewise submit to our Lord and say, "It is God's plan."

Blessings my brother,

Ken

◆ ◆ ◆

Where you live makes no difference as life goes on

"Come now, you who say, 'Today or tomorrow we will go to such and such a city, spend a year there, buy and sell, and make a profit;' whereas you do not know what will happen tomorrow. For what is your life? It is even a vapor that appears for a little time and then vanishes away. Instead you ought to say, 'If the Lord wills, we shall live and do this or that.' " (James 4:13-15)

Most humans never see the inside of a prison, but that does not mean they live free. Instead of bricks and steel bars, their prisons are made of hard hearts, indifference, anger, hatred, laziness, greed, lust, busyness, or any number of other human conditions. The types of prison walls are as different as there are people.

Yet all humans share two things in common.

First, until we die, we all have the same amount of time each day. We cannot save time for tomorrow, nor spend that which we wasted yesterday. In reality, we only have the moment in which we live. It is humbling to think that no matter our station in life, where we live, what we wear, what we do, life goes on with or without us.

Secondly, we all are born into sin and in need of a Savior to restore us to fellowship with God; and that Savior is Jesus Christ.

Only by walking in the light given by Jesus Christ do we understand that, no matter where we live, as life goes on, we can be a productive part of it.

Jesus said, "I am come that they might have life, and that they might have it more abundantly." (John 10:10b) No matter your circumstances, you can live for Him, so that as life goes on, your life will count for Him.

Letter Seventeen:
There is a bomb in Gilead

Genesis 37:25

"As [Joseph's brothers] sat down to eat their meal they looked up and saw a caravan of Ishmaelites coming from Gilead. Their camels were loaded with spices, balm and myrrh, and they were on their way to take them down to Egypt."

Ken,

One of my favorite old spirituals is, "There is a Balm in Gilead." Of course, as a child, when I heard it at my mother's feet, I thought she sang, "There is a bomb in Gilead."

I asked how a bomb could "heal the sin sick soul." She laughed, and explained.

I know that many spiritual songs are not theologically correct; but since my imprisonment, I have come to know not only what Joseph's slavery and imprisonment felt like; but also, what slavery here in the U.S. must have been like — hopeless and helpless. I have learned how there is comfort in the singing of a spiritual that derived from the oppressive slavery era of our history.

"There is a Balm in Gilead," is a hymn that has its inspiration from Jeremiah 8:22, that asks:

> "Is there no balm in Gilead?
> Is there no physician there?
> Why then is there no healing,
> For the wound of My people?"

Gilead was famous for the healing balm. There was good money to be made in Egypt if an Ishmaelite would bring camel-loads of this famous balm extracted from the stems of a tree prevalent in the Gilead area. So it was not surprising that a caravan came by Joseph's brothers that fateful day. But these merchants were not only going to bring a balm to Egypt, they were going to bring a "bomb" to Egypt. This bombshell who they bought and sold was Joseph. He would impact that whole known world.

As the balm for healing came in a small package, so a bombshell for saving Egypt and his own people came in the humble package of the slave, Joseph.

Now, Ken, I'm no Joseph — no bombshell. But occasionally the Lord gives me an opportunity to be a spark. I spoke with a young man yesterday who all his life knew only anger; who acknowledged that his only response to hurt was to hurt back. What a joy it was to see the realization of God's grace hit him in my sharing. "Hit" him is the best way of putting it. As I shared, I saw his face struck by the concept that God doesn't require "pay back" to earn forgiveness. God's grace is freely given.

Sometimes I'm able to share a word to empower someone with the promises of grace. I pray that the Lord gives me courage and confidence to fulfill His purpose for me even though it might be just a spiritual spark.

The balm of Gilead couldn't heal the sin sick souls of Joseph's brothers; but God's forgiveness given by Joseph to his brothers years later was the spiritual balm that healed. A healing balm can be imported into prison through a ministry to outcast convicted fellows. It is a ministry of spiritual healing spoken of in Jeremiah 30:17:

> "But I will restore you to health and heal your wounds,
> declares the Lord because you are called an outcast,

Zion for whom no one cares."

There is a balm in Lansing Correctional Facility that heals the sin sick soul. It is the Gospel of Christ.

To your health,

Tom

◆ ◆ ◆

Tom,

Up north in Minnesota where I was born and raised, we heard "old spirituals" like "There is a Balm in Gilead" only in the movies. Must be a regional thing.

The old spirituals always have simple but catchy tunes, and speak a simple refrain. As children growing up, we can all understand how easy it is to transpose the word "balm" to "bomb," and try to imagine something blowing up in Gilead. We all seem to hear words of destruction easier than words of healing.

I have another view of that old spiritual.
I see in the bomb and the balm two different things producing two different things. A bomb tears down while a balm builds up; a bomb prepares while a balm repairs. But can they "heal the sin sick soul?" By themselves, certainly not, but joined together they do.

The "bombs" of the law prepare our souls for the balm of the gospel. Joseph's imprisonment in Egypt bears this out. Sold into slavery by his brothers, Joseph could have insisted that his anger against them was just and even righteous, but he did not. When he saw his brothers after so many years of wrongful imprisonment, he decided to test their heart by dropping the "bomb" of the law on them, thereby testing their hearts. Joseph could have responded with anger, but hearing their confession he wept instead. He then joyfully poured the balm of grace upon them and gently, as God's Spirit moved him, forgave them of their sins against him.

Yes, for a time I think Joseph felt helpless and I know from time to time you do, too. And though our circumstances are different, we on the outside often feel the same way. But how we respond to that helplessness determines how the balm of Gilead is applied.

So I think we are united with Joseph though suffering. And since we know that life renders to each of us different portions, some suffer more.

Yes, there is much comfort in singing those old spiritual hymns because, in a simple way, they point to Christ. They tell of man's suffering and hint of the believer's joy. They speak of the law which tells us of our sins and failures, and they speak of the gospel which shows us Christ and His righteousness.

Tom, I have thought about that angry young man to whom you ministered. I feel his heart must have felt the bomb and the balm you unloaded and poured upon him. Surely, he realized that it had not been the fault of the people with whom he had lived that he had so often been moved to anger, but the fault of his selfish nature that drove his rage.

I can imagine how his heart rejoiced when, through the balm of Christ's righteousness, the Holy Spirit moved him to real joy. He received forgiveness as your lips declared God's balm, telling this convict that he has been made righteous in Christ; God now sees Christ's sacrifice on the cross in his heart when God looks at it.

It is a wonderful and liberating truth that God sees Christ's death on the cross and not our sins when he looks at our hearts! What joy we have in God's declaration of justice in Christ.

I don't know how long that young man still has to stay in prison, but his anger has been paid for by Christ's suffering, death and resurrection. Now he can look to the future and other things. Every phase of his life and ours are brought into the light of Judgment Day and the glory then to be revealed.

Because we are waiting for our Lord's return, we are diligent in turning away our anger. We guard against the selfish security that characterized the time of Noah (Matt. 24:36ff). We use this beautifully created world without abusing it (1 Cor. 7:31). We regard the sufferings of this present time as light (Rom. 8:18), so light that instead of weeping we rejoice (Luke 6:23). And we are confident of a future life in the midst of death (1 Thes. 4:13-18).

In short, it is the blessed hope of heaven that molds our life on earth.

Tom, indeed you are a bombshell of Christ in Lansing because the bomb you dropped on the heart of that angry young man and the balm you poured upon him was the law and the gospel of our Lord Jesus Christ. Yes, there is a balm in Lansing Correctional Facility that heals the sin sick soul. It is the Gospel of Christ. And Christ was delivered to that soul by a "bombshell" that unloaded the balm of Zion.

Love you brother,

Ken

◆ ◆ ◆

Getting Balmed

"And do not be drunk with wine, in which is dissipation; but be filled with the Spirit..." (Ephesians 5:18)

Searching for peace, comfort, a way to fight off trouble, many turn to excessive use of alcohol or mind-altering drugs. Paul tells us there is a better way.

Jesus called the Holy Spirit a Comforter — a balm. As our Comforter, the Holy Spirit speaks peace to us through the Word of God.

Luke 5:31-32, "Jesus answered and said to them, 'Those who are well have no need of a physician, but those who are sick. I have not come to call the righteous, but sinners, to repentance.'" Jesus is the Surgeon who has come to rescue a sin sick soul from destruction and damnation and to send His Comforter to bring peace.

You say, "But I am not good enough to go to Jesus."

Jesus came to call people like you to Him. He set no preconditions. He put faith in your heart so that you could believe on Him and have eternal life.

Do you want real peace? Do you want real comfort? Do you want real healing? With a simple prayer from your heart, go to the One who will fill you with His Spirit; go to His Word, and He will apply the right type and amount of balm to bring you everlasting comfort. There is no other way to get balmed.

There is a balm in Gilead
An African-American Spiritual

There is a balm in Gilead
To make the wounded whole;
There is a balm in Gilead
To heal the sin sick soul.

Some times I feel discouraged,
And think my work's in vain,
But then the Holy Spirit
Revives my soul again.

If you can't preach like Peter,
If you can't pray like Paul,
Just tell the love of Jesus,
And say He died for all.

Letter Eighteen:
Shackles for Shekels

Genesis 37:28

"So when the Midianite merchants came by, [Joseph's] brothers pulled him up out of the cistern and sold him for twenty shekels of silver to the Ishmaelites who took him to Egypt."

Ken,

Joseph's brothers made a good deal, Ken. They didn't have Joseph's blood on their hands and made a quick 20 shekels of silver to boot. I am sure that the caravan merchants turned a good profit in Egypt when they resold Joseph there.

Plodding along in a neck iron and leg shackles, Joseph became a commodity to be bought and sold for a price, plus shipping and handling. He felt the agonizing realization that he was one moment a brother/son, the next moment a slave. He was suddenly a piece of merchandise much like the spices and myrrh these traveling entrepreneurs packed to Egypt.

Ken, sometimes I am gripped by the horrendous feeling that I am just a commodity. While the stock market drops, the prison building industry holds true and private prisons seem to flourish. While I am not in a private prison, this state prison has a private medical service, a private food service, privately run programs (sex offenders, drug addiction) and private educational services. These all have an ideal profit situation. Their profit margin is determined by the least amount of food or medicine given per inmate population and by the federal dollars granted per inmate in their program.

Now I have been given an inmate number and warehoused in this prison setting where fortunes flourish at the expense of inmates. There are a lot of hands in the shekel kitty in the prison business. I and the other 2 million plus inmates in the nation's prisons and jails are important commodities affecting the economy.

When I feel most like a market commodity, I stop and think that I and other sinners have been bought with a price: Not with gold or silver but with the precious blood of our Lord and Savior Jesus Christ. By His blood I am no longer an inventory item number crammed in a sardine-like cell; but I am free-redeemed. The Lord owns me and by faith, I am His servant.

It was no accident that the price for Joseph as a slave was the price for redeeming a person his age dedicated to the Lord by a special vow. Leviticus 27:1-5, "If anyone makes a special vow to dedicate persons to the Lord by giving equivalent values…if it is a person between the ages of 5 and 20, set the value of a male at 20 shekels."

What is a life worth, Ken?

The 10 brothers of Joseph would have each received two shekels share of the slave money while watching Joseph in shackles shuffle off South. They would have never guessed the ironic twist many years later when Joseph, with a snap of his fingers, "gave to Benjamin [his innocent little brother] 300 silver shekels." (Genesis 45:22)

What a contrast! The man sold for 20 shekels gives away 300! This is all just nickels and dimes when I think that our Savior was sold out for 30 pieces of silver. He who for our sake became poor so that we might be rich.

Thanks for listening.

Yours in Christ,

Tom

◆ ◆ ◆

Tom,

As I read various commentaries on Genesis 37, I was reminded again that God values men over manna — an idea that you touched upon in your last letter.

I know that I have often left the impression that all of Joseph's brothers acted with malice and treated him like a beast of burden. That's simply not true.

Benjamin, the youngest of the 12, was not even involved in the conspiracy, being around five years old at the time. Two of the other brothers, who eventually played a part in selling Joseph to the Ishmaelites for 20 shekels, at first showed that they valued their younger brother. Reuben had saved Joseph's life (v. 21) and Judah tried to save Joseph's life by convincing his brothers to sell Joseph to the Ishmaelites rather than kill him (v. 26).

None of this, however, made any impression upon the other brothers. They were determined to get rid of Joseph. They dipped his coat in the blood of a goat and sent it to his father saying, "We have found this; see whether it is your son's coat or not." Jacob mourned bitterly. He had to live with the thought that his favored son had been devoured by a wild beast — he would never again see him.

But while Jacob mourned, the brothers sold Joseph into slavery. Joseph was humiliated, but according to the wonderful counsel of God, he would eventually be exalted.

Luther made a comparison here: "For as Isaiah (53:8) says of Christ, 'He was cut off out of the land of the living, so also Joseph is removed from the land and sight of his father, just as if he would never return to his father or see him again.' "

Yes, Jacob's other sons sold Joseph for 20 shekels of silver, but look at the results of their evil. Luke wrote in Acts 7:9-10; "And the patriarchs became jealous of Joseph and sold him into Egypt. And yet God was with him, and rescued him from all his afflictions, and granted him favor and wisdom in the sight of Pharaoh, King of Egypt; and he made him Governor over Egypt and his entire household."

Tom, it is good for us to review these texts for in them we receive comfort for our own lives. In good times and in bad, we look to the past and see how God valued His creation to provide good times for us in the present — and the best of times for us in the future.

In bad times, our faith moves us to remember that God especially valued man when He personally breathed into him the breath of life and created him in His image. Jesus then elevated our value when He compared man to the birds of the air, saying, "are you not of more value than they?" (Matthew 6:26)

Then Jesus lifted us up to the utmost value when He died on the cross to forgive us of our sins and gave eternal life to all who believe. Jesus loved us so much that He commanded us to value ourselves when He said, "love your neighbor as yourself."

In your last letter you wrote, "The Lord owns me and by faith I am His servant." This is the confession of a man who knows the Lord and the Lord knows him. But, like Joseph, you have been brought down low and have been cut off from the sight of your father, family and friends.

The fact that you have so many friends tells me that you live out the command of God, to love your neighbor as yourself. Still, you must constantly fight against the nagging thought that you have no value in life, or that you give anything of value back to life. I sometimes think the same thing of myself. Surely, it is common to man.

And I also know that you have been visited with many afflictions while in prison, but look what God has done. He has allowed you to be placed in prison because He so highly values the many souls there that He has touched them with the saving Gospel of Jesus Christ through your lips.

God is with you and granted you favor and wisdom in the sight of many. And by faith, He has made you a son and a king in the household of God. He has esteemed you in the eyes of many of your "brothers."

For we see you as a good friend and a humble son of the King. Those earthly views may not be strong enough to set you free from

Lansing's walls, but God's grace in Christ Jesus has freed you already and has declared you a valuable child in His kingdom.

Of greatest value,

Ken

◆ ◆ ◆

What's your value?

"For God so loved the world [you], that He gave His only begotten Son; that whoever [you] believes in Him should not perish, but have everlasting life." John 3:16

In some ways, all people are commodities to be bought, sold or traded for value.

Babies generate income for doctors, nurses, hospitals, and a lifetime of suppliers of goods — clothing, education, transportation, entertainment.

Students from kindergarten to high school provide raw material for the education industry that requires annual spending of hundreds of billions of dollars. College students create a market for higher education. Trade schools and apprenticeship programs profit while training future employees.

Employers mark up the costs of paying employees to establish a selling price for their goods and services. Governments raise their income by taxing their residents.

Anyone who knows what a funeral costs knows that even in death, your remains are valuable.

You are worth a lot of money, no matter your state in life — but this is not your true value.

Your true value is this: Jesus Christ died for your sins and rose again to sit at the right hand of God. When Jesus paid the ultimate price for you, He showed how much God values and loves you, and because of this, you can know you have eternal life with Him. "And this is the testimony: that God has given us eternal life, and this life is in His Son. He who has the Son has life; he who does not have the Son of God does not have life." (I John 5:11-12)

You may see yourself as worthless. That is simply not so. You are worth every drop of the precious blood of Jesus Christ. Confess Him as your Savior today.

Letter Nineteen:
Letting Go of Your Benjamin

Genesis 43:11-14

"Then their father Israel said to them. 'If it must be, then do this...take your brother also and go back to the man at once...if I am bereaved, I am bereaved.' "

Ken,

A dear brother in the Lord, Calvin, a retired pastor and now volunteer prison chapel choir director, helped me out during one of my low times when he shared with me his message about Israel letting go of Benjamin in the saga of Joseph. It moved me to contemplate these thoughts.

Ken, at the risk of you making a joke about my name being "Bird," I want to share with you that I am having troubles with what many people would call the "Empty Nest Syndrome." My case may be an extreme condition because I had to raise my daughter and two sons while in prison. Now they are adults-going their own way.

My daughter is in the Marines in Okinawa. One son is now married and lives hundreds of miles away. And my youngest son has moved to France. Almost 20 time zones and two barbed wire fences separate me from by children.

As it was difficult to give up my children when they were young; it is so much more painful to give them up as adults. For me, and so many prison inmates, visits with family are encouraging and exhilarating. But the goodbyes are heart-wrenching as you watch your family walk away and the gate shuts behind them.

So I have felt the hurt of Israel when he let go of Benjamin. Joseph had told the brothers not to come back to Egypt unless they brought back Benjamin, the youngest (and only innocent) brother. Israel, who had never recovered from the loss of Joseph, could not bear the thought of losing Benjamin. But other options were not available. If the family did not go to Egypt at the height of the seven-year famine, they would all starve. If they went to Egypt without Benjamin, they would get no food from Joseph.

Israel had to let go of Benjamin. It was unavoidable. More significantly, it was God's plan. Ken, we all sometime in our life to some degree or another have to "let go of our Benjamins." In my case, I had to let go of my children. I have to let go of my family and friends every visit. I have to often let go of my pride, my masculinity, and my bitterness.

Israel let go of Benjamin saying, "If I am bereaved, I am bereaved." What Israel did not let go of was a firm grip on his faith in the Lord. Israel says, as he lets go of Benjamin, "And may God Almighty grant you mercy…to return."

We must let go of our Benjamins, but never our faith. The Father promises His abiding mercy in Christ so that we may hold on.

In Him,

Tom

◆ ◆ ◆

Tom,

"Letting go of Benjamin" is a particularly sad story because it affects the institution of marriage. One day in our life we will all experience this loss — some to a greater degree than others.
The "Empty Nest Syndrome" — parents seeing their children leave home or children experiencing the death of parents — really doesn't

capture adequately the emotional pain and stress that lies in the hearts of those left behind. An element of emotion to this euphemism is worthwhile if we are to appreciate the agonizing loneliness of the empty nest.

Jacob brings that desired emotion to his empty nest. In verse 14, Jacob prays, "May God almighty grant you mercy before the man," and then he cries out, "If I am bereaved of my children, I am bereaved."

He lost Joseph many years earlier and now he thinks he will lose Simeon who is presently held captive in Egypt. He surmises that he will lose Benjamin as well. So he despairs of letting Benjamin go, and he fights against his son's request to take Benjamin back to Egypt where he will face "the man."

What an irony of agony!

But faith conquers. Jacob lets go of Benjamin, handing him over to Judah. He neither despairs nor curses but resolves in his heart, "I have resisted you and have wanted to try everything rather than send my dearly beloved son to Egypt. I did not want to tempt God, and for this reason I sought various means to avoid bringing him into danger. Now, since we are driven by extreme famine in the land, I will entrust him to God's predestination and goodness."

Luther writes, "For when we have done all that was possible in our tribulation and distress — just as Jacob opposed the wishes of his sons with great zeal — and there has been no help in those means, then indeed we should say, 'Well and good! I have done what I could. I have not tempted God. As for the rest, I must rely on the promise He has given and entrust everything to His will and good pleasure.' "

Tom, in faith Jacob did let go and so have you. You have done all that you can while in prison. You baptized your children and placed a Bible in their hands. You fought for them through your parents. You sought to get them in a Christian home. You wrote them Godly advice and encouraged them in the Lord Jesus. You fervently prayed daily for their spiritual welfare. You called them on the telephone and they visit you. You loved them and they loved you and that love remains and grows in them to this day. Yes, their material needs were taken care of by others, but during these years, they were denied the gracious message of the Gospel as a result of Arkansas mandating their place of dwelling. This was beyond your wishes and control.

So you did all you could and there was little help in all this.

I understand when you write that we must let our Benjamins go, you are saying, "Well and good! I have done what I could. I have not tempted God. As for the rest, I must rely on the promise He has given and entrust everything to His will and good pleasure."

There was another "letting go" that makes our affliction bearable; when God let go of His Son on the Cross. He had to let go of His only beloved Jesus. On the Cross, Jesus cried out to His Father, "My God, My God, why have you forsaken me?" (Mark 15:34).

But God had to let go of Jesus, let Him die so that we can be brought to God through Jesus. That divine act of mercy, through the merits of Christ's death on the cross, that we grasp by faith, frees us sinners from the guilt and penalties of sin. The penalty of our sin is now paid in full. Christ died for all (John 3:16) and whosoever believes in Him shall not perish but have everlasting life.

We who God pardoned are justified in that we are declared innocent, being placed in a position of not having broken the Law and not deserving punishment. Such forgiveness is granted to believers as a free gift (Ephesians 2:8). It is a gift of the mercy of God to which the sinner receives (2 Corinthians 5:19)

Yes Tom you "... have felt the hurt of Israel [Jacob] when he let go of Benjamin." But what he and you did not let go of was your firm grip of faith in the Lord. And as you say, "We must let go of our Benjamins, but never our faith."

Blessings,

Ken

◆ ◆ ◆

But never separated...ever

"For I am persuaded, that neither death nor life, nor angels nor principalities, nor powers, nor things present nor things to come, nor height nor depth, nor any other created thing, shall be able to separate us from the love of God which is in Christ Jesus our Lord." (Romans 8:38-39)

In prison, greetings are passionate. Kisses linger. Tight hugs are normal. Departures evidence a mixture of sadness and fatalism, an unwillingness to let go, because of the physical separation of the inmate from his guests, and the knowledge that awaiting him or her are walls, jailer's keys and a routine over which he or she has no control.

Outside of prison, our separations are often not that different from those of inmates. Our children and friends visit, and they leave. Once out of our home, we do not know where their steps or decisions will take them. And the noise of a busy house is replaced with the sound of silence. As we grow older, loneliness can become our prison.

For those who walk in Christ, though, physical separation offers a unique and different perspective. If loved ones also walk in faith, there remains a bond and the joy of knowing that God goes with them, and we can say, "Godspeed." But if they reject faith, our hearts are burdened with sadness, and we pray daily that Jesus Christ will send His Spirit to quicken them, to bring them to Himself.

Do you feel separated from family and friends? Hebrews 13:5b says, "For He Himself has said, 'I will never leave you, nor forsake you." So if we are believers in Jesus Christ, we can never really be alone or be separated. We are united with those we love in the bond of Christ, no matter our circumstances.

At times of sending away, we can say, as did King David to his son Solomon, "...Be strong and of good courage, and do it; do not fear nor be dismayed, for the LORD God — my God — will be with you; He will not leave you nor forsake you, until you have finished all the work for the service of the house of the LORD." (I Chronicles 28:20)

And as He blesses our children and loved ones in their absence, we know that He remains our constant companion.

Letter Twenty:
Yearn to Learn

Psalm 105:17-22

"[The Lord] sent a man before them — Joseph, sold as a slave, they bruised his feet with shackles, his neck was put in irons till what he foretold came to pass, till the word of the Lord proved him."

Ken,

Someone once said, "The only lesson people learn from history is that people do not learn from history." Acute, but a little negative. Yet we both understand that all men by nature are sinful, including myself. So people, bound in sin, are bound to not learn from history.

For 3½ years, I worked in the Prison's Admissions and Discharge Department. My duties consisted of doing some of the paperwork and outfitting all the men who arrived or departed the prison. I was appalled to see so many men paroled to life out "on the streets" and then a month or two or maybe a year later, those same men return back to prison for violations of their parole. So many men came back that I concluded that the only lesson that people learn from prison is that people do not learn from prison.

Yet, Ken, I have had the privilege of sharing God's Word with some of the most vicious, perverted criminals. They were struck by the terror of God's wrath against sin and then comforted by the discovery of forgiveness in Christ. Such men yearn to learn from

God's Word, from prison and from history.

A group of us inmates sat around "the yard" talking about a beautiful and valuable historical Psalm 105. "And [the Lord] sent a man before [the people of Israel], Joseph, sold as a slave...his neck was put in irons till what he foretold came to pass, till the word of the Lord proved him."

We learned from the Psalm, two of the most valuable lessons. The first is that no matter how bleak life looks, God is still about the business of fulfilling His plans. At many stages along the path of Joseph's life, everything looked hopeless for this young man. But God had a big plan and it was going to come to pass.

The second lesson our little group of convicts gleaned could be summed up in this little story: Once upon a time there was an inmate who was released from prison. He went off on a personal spiritual quest for an answer to the question of the secret to life. He had heard that there was an ex-con, the convict of convicts, who stood 6'4", 300 pounds in solid bulk, hairless except a long Fu Manchu. So our released prisoner braved churning seas, vicious winds, bitter cold, dangerous mountainous terrain, to reach the inmate's shrine. Battered and bruised, with barely a breath, he asked the great convict of convicts, "What is the secret of life?" With wise words, yet brief, the con of cons proclaimed, "Don't ever trust anybody!"

Well, Ken, the real secret to life could have been more simply found in the historical Psalm of Israel (105) that contains the story of Joseph and others. The lesson for those who yearn to learn is, "The Lord our God...remembers His covenant forever, and the word He commanded, for a thousand generations (v. 8)."

Don't trust humans; trust in the Lord.

Trusting Him,

Tom

Tom,

It is encouraging to all people of good will when rehabilitation takes place no matter where it takes place. The fact that you are able to bring Biblical teaching to fellow inmates gives welcome significance to your prison life.

What a great idea it is to study Biblical history. Psalms 105 and 106 give us poetically the summary of Israel's history. This particular history focuses on the miraculous delivery of the children of Israel out of Egypt. We see that when Israel learned from humans they were punished; when they yearned to learn from God, they were blessed.

The two points that you and your fellow believers gleaned from your study are applicable to sinners everywhere — namely, that God is faithful to carry out His plans, and, "Don't trust humans, trust in the Lord."

It is a pity that some refuse to learn from history, like the "con of convicts" of your letter. These kind of people know the idea well enough — that those who fail to learn the lessons of history are damned to repeat it — but they do not know the key point you made about the role of sin in history. They do not accept the proposition that sin is the cause of harmful history repeating itself. But we know by faith that history repeats itself because sin drives the man who does not trust God and as long as it does, his history will repeat itself.

Your Bible study with fellow believers summed up the part of history that went unlearned by the great "con of convicts." The difference between him and us is not that he is a sinner and we are not, for we are all sinners. The difference is that we sinners in Christ yearn to learn.

Perhaps, the great con was right from a purely human perspective when he said, "Don't ever trust anybody!" But he was spiritually wrong. He would have been able to shed his indignant ways had he yearned to learn the truth of life's secret: "Don't trust humans; trust in the Lord."

I, too, place myself in the word "They" — that group with

whom you were privileged to share the Gospel. "They were struck by the terror of God's wrath against sin and then comforted by the discovery of forgiveness in Christ."

We (all those for whom Christ prayed in the Garden of Gethsemane), however, yearn to learn about our sin and, even more so, of the forgiveness of sins by faith in Christ.

Luther tells of Jacobs' ten sons trying to cover up their sin of selling Joseph (Gen. 42:34). However, unknown to the brothers, Joseph is trying to expose their sin by requiring them to bring Benjamin to him. During their journey toward home, they discovered the cup and money that Joseph had planted in the sacks on their donkeys, and they were terrified. Luther compares this to God exposing all our sin at the cross of Christ.

"We see that the same thing happens in the household and in the state; for whatever sin is committed, this is thrown back on no one, because no one easily allows his evil deeds to be made known and censured. They are all pious; no one wants to admit that he has done wrong...Who, then, has sinned? Who will make expiation? The Son of God alone is the sinner. No one else. He alone bears the sin and says (Ps. 51:1): 'Have mercy on Me, because I have sinned against Thee.' He acknowledges and confesses sin in earnest, not for His own Person, which is holy and righteous, but as a Pleader and Advocate before the Judge; and He renders satisfaction for us."

Believers in Christ do not argue about why God has permitted evil to visit us. Rather, we ask how we can be set free from evil.

Luther wrote, "We know that God speaks with us to arouse us to acknowledge sin. When it has been acknowledged, He says: 'Your sins are forgiven you; take heart, My son,' (Matt. 9:2) because I have given My Son as a Lamb that is spotless from the beginning. If you acknowledge and confess your iniquity and transgressions, then My Son will be the propitiation for your sins; He will be your sanctification, redemption, righteousness, and wisdom. (1 Cor. 1:30)

"God is wonderful in His saints (Ps. 68:35). To Him they are at the same time both righteous and unrighteous. And God is wonderful in the hypocrites. To Him they are at the same time both unrighteous and righteous. For inasmuch as the saints are always aware of their sin and seek righteousness from God in accord with His mercy, for this very reason they are always also regarded as righteous by God. Thus in their own sight and in truth they are unrighteous, but before God they are righteous because He reckons them so because of their confession of sin.

"They are actually sinners, but they are righteous by the imputation of a merciful God. They are unknowingly righteous and knowingly unrighteous; they are sinners in fact but righteous in hope." (Luther, Vol. 25, p 258)

It is a misfortune that the "great con of convicts" did not yearn to learn that the Son of God alone is the sinner; for if he had he would have come to understand and by God's grace believe what you and your fellow Christians professed among yourselves — "trust in the Lord."

Herein lies the whole history of mankind for those who yearn to learn.

A fellow student,

Ken

♦ ♦ ♦

Who can you trust?

"Trust in the LORD with all your heart, and lean not on your own understanding; In all your ways acknowledge Him, and He shall direct your paths." (Proverbs 3:5-6)

Do you really want to stay out of trouble and live at peace? Do you want to make wise choices?

John Donne wrote, "No man is an island." He meant that no one can live without contact or connection to other people. It seems impossible that you can live without trusting at least one or two other persons, unless you choose to live secluded and alone. Yet, if you trust people, at some point they will fail you — and you will fail them.

If, however, you look to God in prayer and to His Word for guidance, He will lead you to trustworthy people, and show you how to be trusted. Always remember that humans are prone to sin, and at various times, still will disappoint and fail you.

The greatness of living by faith in Jesus Christ and seeking Him in daily prayer and Bible study is that the more you know about Him, the more you want to know about Him. And the more you know Him, the more personal He becomes to you. And the more personal He becomes, the more you trust Him.

The "con of cons" had it right for those who try to find life's meaning and satisfaction in human relationships — never trust anyone. But had he learned one essential lesson, he could have been spared the criminal's life. And that lesson is found in a promise made by Jesus, where He said as recorded in Matthew 6:33, "But seek first the kingdom of God and his righteousness, and all these things shall be added to you."

John wrote that Jesus "...knew what was in man." (John 2:25) There is no one who can "con" Him, and He "cons" no one.

You *can* trust Jesus, the Son of God.

Letter Twenty-One:
Body Disposition Form

Genesis 50:25-26

"Then Joseph took an oath of the sons of Israel, saying: God will visit you, and you shall carry up my bones from here. So Joseph died, being a hundred and ten years old; and they embalmed him, and he was put in a coffin in Egypt."

Ken,

I was called down to my cell house Unit Team Counselor's office today. Usually that means having a review of my custody and classification status or filling out some paperwork formalities such as telephone list update or visiting list update. The unit team counselor slid two forms across his desk for me to fill out. The paperwork took me by surprise.

One was a living will kind of form. It spoke of a "do not resuscitate" clause and do not take "extreme measures" to preserve life in case the decision need arise.

The second form was a "Body Removal Form."

In shock, I asked the Unit Team man, "Do you know something I don't know?" Maybe I was terminally ill and they forgot to tell me.

But the counselor sheepishly mumbled, "Naw, this is just a new form for us to have on file, you know, just in case."

This body removal form was a multiple choice form which gave me three options of what to do with my body just in case I died in here: One, the family takes my body for interment; two, my body be donated to Kansas University School of Medicine; three, cremation at the state's expense.

So, Ken, I had to confront the thought that I could die in prison and decide what to do with my body. Frankly, I don't really care how they dispose of my body. But I wondered about Joseph.

It was of utmost importance to him to have his body transported to the Promised Land. Though he was second in command of all of Egypt and he had anything he wanted in this richest of kingdoms, there was one thing Egypt did not have — the Promised Land of God.

Joseph knew he did not belong in Egypt. Joseph knew that his body would not rest in peace until he was brought "home." Joseph was carried away from home as a slave and therefore, it was his utmost desire to be carried back home as a free man.

For hundreds of years Joseph's body was preserved by Egyptian embalmers and when Pharaoh let God's people go with Moses in the great exodus, "Moses took the bones of Joseph with him…" (Exodus 13:19)

For 40 years of wandering the wilderness, the people of Israel carried the body of Joseph. The other sons of Israel, the generation of the people of the exodus, and even Moses himself, were not buried in the Promised Land. But "Joseph's bones which the Israelites had brought up from Egypt were buried at Shechem in the tract of land that Jacob bought…" (Joshua 24:33)

So what about my bones, Ken?

If Egypt was the symbol of slavery and the Promised Land the symbol of freedom for Joseph; then I think that cremation or donation would be symbols of imprisonment where my body belongs to the state.

Sending my body to my family would symbolize that my soul has been set free. I would like even the disposal of my body to be a witness that the Lord has set me free from sin and Hell.

Heaven is my home.

In Him,

Tom

♦ ♦ ♦

Tom,

The subject of death can be frightening. In his natural rational state, no man wants to die, so when you raised the issue of death you opened a can of fright.

On occasion, I will ask parishioners to consider with me their personal wishes for a funeral service. I ask, "What hymns would you like sung? What Scripture passages would you like read? And who would you like as your pallbearers?" Invariably they look surprised, then sad, and after that, speechless. Most of them don't want to talk about death or even think about it.

In fact, it was just recently that I have given thought to preparing for my own funeral. I, too, fear physical death. I fear it because I recognize my own mortality and the dreadful thought of hell. And the same time, I do not fear death, because I know that Jesus died for my sins and promised me a mansion in heaven.

A few years ago a man walked off the street and into my office — I will call him Jack. Jack told me that he had been baptized a Missouri Synod Lutheran; that he had fallen away from faith; that he lived a worldly and adulterous life. The doctor discovered that Jack had inoperable cancer and expected him to die within six months. Faced with death, Jack wanted to join the Church, receive forgiveness and partake of Holy Communion.

After four weeks of studying the Bible and *Luther's Small Catechism*, Redeemer received him as a member. Two weeks before Jack died, he called me to his home — he lay in bed, soon to die. He insisted that his atheist wife be there because he had something to say that he wanted her to hear. He looked at her as he spoke to me, "Pastor, I do not want to be cremated. I want a Christian burial." His wife planned to have him cremated and I knew it. So I came prepared.

The Bible does not forbid cremation, although it never speaks of it positively. Pagan Rome often burned the bones of the dead, as did the Hindus and Greeks. The Creator of life regarded cremation as loathsome. (Amos 2:1; Joshua 7:25; Lev 20:14).

On judgment day, the Lord Jesus Christ will Himself raise up the body and return it to the souls that are presently with Him in Paradise. To the living, it leaves a physical reminder so that when they go to the cemetery and look at the grave they can say, "When Christ returns, He will raise up that dirt and make it glorious and incorruptible." The bodies of the children of Israel were buried (Gen. 23:19; 25:9) and God personally buried Moses. And Joseph of Arimathea buried God in Jerusalem some 2000 years ago.

Tom, I thought you would enjoy reading again the comforting words Luther wrote concerning the resurrection as it relates to Genesis 50:25: "Then Joseph took an oath of the sons of Israel, saying: God will visit you, and you shall carry up my bones from here."

"Here Joseph declares his faith when he desires to be among those who were to be raised with Christ. And I believe that he returned to life along with the other saints of whom mention is made in Matt. 27:52-53. Indeed, he wants to rest in the land of Canaan, even though the place and the burial are of little importance. For he could have been buried in Egypt, and it would not have been difficult for Christ to raise the fathers from Egypt or from anywhere else. But in order to bear witness to his faith in Christ he gives orders that his bones be borne down to the land of Canaan. For he also knew that the people of Israel were to be multiplied in the land promised to their fathers. Therefore he wants that tomb to be before the eyes of all his descendants, in order that his children and grandchildren may remember their father and their ancestors and, in accordance with their example, may persevere in the same faith and promise in which he had fallen asleep with his fathers." (LW Vol. 8)

Yes, Tom, I share your confession: "Sending my body to my family would symbolize that my soul has been set free. I would like even the disposal of my body to be a witness that the Lord has set me free from sin and Hell. Heaven is my home."

Should you go to Heaven before me, I shall come to see your remains lying in that grave and remember. And should I precede you, I pray that you will come to my gravesite and remember — the resurrection unto everlasting life.

By the way, Jack's atheistic wife finally approved of her husband's request for burial. He was buried on the third day following his death.

Blessings in Christ,

Ken

◆ ◆ ◆

Disposing of man's soul

"And Jesus said unto him, 'Assuredly, I say to you, today you shall be with me in Paradise.'" (Luke 23:43)

Jesus spoke these words to the thief who hung next to Him on his own cross. That thief had just confessed his guilt moments earlier, and rebuked the other criminal who hung on Jesus' other side. The repentant thief knew he hung next to God's Son, the One who could give him eternal life.

The repentant thief's body may have ended up being cremated in a garbage pit, but his soul rose to heaven along with that of his Savior, Jesus. He had no question where he would spend eternity, because Jesus had paid his sin sentence for him. Jesus disposed of the man's soul by welcoming him to heaven.

Bodies are rightfully called "remains." All that remains is the earthly temple which quickly turns to dust, and much is said about how best to dispose of that body. But for those who, by the faith Christ has implanted in their hearts, confess Him as Savior, there can be no question of the disposition of their soul for all eternity.

"O Death, where is your sting? O Hades, where is your victory? The sting of death is sin, and the strength of sin is the law. But thanks be to God, who gives us the victory through our Lord Jesus Christ." (I Corinthians 15:55-57)

In Christ, the believer has a certain disposition — in heaven at the throne of God.

Letter Twenty-Two:
The Law of the Jungle

Gen 39:20b-21a

"But while Joseph was there in prison, the Lord was with him: He showed him kindness."

Ken,

Danger! You ask about how dangerous is prison life. Well, Ken, you must disregard much of the horror stories that so popularly portray prison life in the movies and on TV. There are not rampant stabbings and beatings nor is there constant unchecked attacks by sexual predators. But these things do go on, for sure.

There is always the possibility of being in the wrong place at the wrong time saying the wrong thing to the wrong person. But in my years in prison, the Lord has been with me and protected me.

There are convict traps that involve gambling, debts and inevitable violence, and so I avoid the traps.

It is much like the law of the jungle in here. Violent and sexual predators in prison work much like the animal kingdom predators. They watch the herd and look for the young, the weak and the isolated to stalk and attack.

A sanctuary. It was Christmas Eve just before a Convicts for Christ worship service that I rediscovered the original meaning of "sanctuary" for a young boy named Jimmy. A few inmates had gathered, yet scattered in various pockets of chairs in the auditorium as I was talking to the pianist about the order of the Christmas Eve service. I glanced up to see a young man slide into the back in the semidarkness of the room.

Seconds later, I saw two heads poke through the door of the foyer. I recognized them as known homosexual predators. In prison, you don't know what is going on as much as you sense what is going on. I sensed it.

I walked up to the young man in the back row. As we introduced each other, I found out his name was Jimmy. I saw a black left eye and a swollen bottom lip. Jimmy was tense. Trouble had found him once that night and he was hoping that trouble would not find him again. The homosexual predators were after him. Trapped and vulnerable on this Christmas Eve, Jimmy hoped that the chapel was going to be his sanctuary.

I stepped out into the foyer to face the predators and I saw a third one outside the door acting as jigger (lookout for guards coming). Now either one of these predators and certainly both could easily have beaten me down physically. But this chapel was a sanctuary and the Lord was with me. I said, "Not here; not now."

Maybe these two knew the Lord was with me or maybe just because I was an old timer, maybe because they respected the sincerity of my faith over the years in prison. One turned and muttered, "Later." They left.

Jimmy worshiped with us. Then I talked with him after the service. I shared with him that I would stand by him; but because he lived in a different unit, I could not be with him all the time and that he would have to stand up for himself. It was a moment of truth.

Would he go back to his Unit or would he seek the shelter of the special protective custody unit? I shared that the Lord would be with him.

We had just worshiped "Immanuel," which means, "God is with us." Jimmy decided that he thought it best if God would go with him as he checked into the Protective Custody Unit. I walked with him to the shift office, shook his hand, blessed him with the peace of the Lord, and I never saw him again.

I'm glad that the chapel that Christmas Eve night was a sanctuary for young Jimmy. I know that the Lord was with Joseph for all his years in prison. Immanuel was God with me on that fearful Christmas Eve and throughout the years in here.

In Christ,

Tom

◆ ◆ ◆

Tom,

I cannot imagine the dangers of prison life. That is why I found your Christmas Eve experience with Jimmy so frightening. Certainly the presence and kindness of the Lord accounts for your protection and his. It is disturbing that Jimmy must live by the law of the jungle and live in fear of sexual predators. I suppose he may need to take drastic action and even be prepared to fight to the death to defend himself, or he'll become a regular victim. The law of the jungle ruled that night as homosexual predators sought their prey; and yet in the sanctuary you were able to tell Jimmy of Immanuel — that "God with us" is also our Sanctuary.

I must say that of all the dangers of prison life, the thought of homosexual rape frightens me the most. To be violated in such a violent and deviant way might well drive me to despair of life, where later I might need to plead my case before the merciful God. But you stepped in, Tom, and your intervention helped and protected Jimmy with might and Word.

As you said, "the Lord has been with me and protected me." He certainly did that night and you are living proof of His living faithfulness to believers.

Luther reminds us that God is like a kind father who steps in and settles our quarrels for the safety of all. He desires that all people be defended and protected from the hatred and hostility of others. That's why He has given us the Fifth Commandment to serve as our fortress and refuge — so that no one may harm a neighbor. Yet we know that Christ also died on the cross for the homosexual.

A few years ago I conducted a funeral service for a 38-year old homosexual who died from complications of AIDS. About a month before he died, his sister asked me to minister to him. She is a member of my congregation, so I did. As I entered his hospital room, his lover sat in a chair near a window, just 15 feet away and heard our conversation.

I turned to Bill and explained that Christ Jesus died on Calvary's cross to forgive the sins of the whole world, including the sin of homosexuality. I let him know that as long as he remained in that sin he has no hope of forgiveness or eternal life, but only the horrors of hell awaited him.

I saw real terror in his eyes. Then he whispered to me of his guilt-ridden conscience, of his fear of hell and the wrath of God. I joyfully announced to him the grace of God. I told him that Christ has redeemed him from all of his sins, from death and from the power of the devil; that He has taken away all his guilt and suffered all his punishment; and that He has freed him from the slavery of sin. And by the grace of God, Bill confessed his sin and faith in Jesus Christ as his personal Savior. Two weeks later, Bill died.

Bill's funeral was joyous. And the Lord kindly took Bill into Paradise.

When I read Luther on Genesis 30:20ff, I remembered your Christmas Eve experience and mine, although yours was quite different and dangerous. I thought of how God, as the Bishop of our souls, sees, cares and is mindful of our work and especially His "Modern Day Joseph" in prison.

Luther writes, "Christ, the Bishop of souls (1 Peter 2:25) who is mindful of hell and death, is the ONLY ONE who sees Joseph, the ONLY ONE who cares about Him...Therefore when all things seem hopeless, and no help or comfort is left, then the help of the Lord begins. He says: 'Behold, I am present, Joseph; let it be enough for you that I am mindful of you.'

"Accordingly...'The Lord was with Joseph' — is full of consolation and joy. For although he is not yet liberated, God is nevertheless already thinking about raising him up from death and hell after his blood has cried long enough to heaven (Gen. 4:10) and has brought it about that the Lord became the Bishop of his soul and inclined His mercy to him." (Luther, Vol. 7)

That Christmas Eve in prison, the Lord stood with you. He sustained you in disgrace and confusion, and inspired in you this feeling: "Do not fear; let your heart be strengthened; wait for the Lord!"

Your brother in Christ,

Ken

◆ ◆ ◆

Strong defense; strong offense

"Watch, stand fast in the faith, be brave, be strong. Let all that you do be done with love." I Corinthians 16:13-14

Life requires being sensitive to what is going on around us. God created our bodies with great instinctual defense mechanisms that alert us to physical danger; He has, likewise, given us His Holy Spirit to alert us to spiritual danger. So we must watch at all times; be on guard for the Evil One who prowls about, "seeking whom he may devour." (I Peter 5:8)

Our source of strength to stand against all that might attack us is the power God grants, that is, if we have reverential fear of Him. So we trust Him because He is strong, certainly far stronger than we are; we trust Him because He first loved us; we trust Him because He sacrificed His own Son for our salvation.

But as we stand fast in the face of grave danger we must also be brave, willing to assert the strength that God gives us. We cannot cower, nor show weakness, because our attacker will sense it immediately. And this is one of the parodies of being a Christian; Christians who live their lives under the influence of the Word and the Spirit are very strong people, not weak, as the culture tries to portray.

By being watchful, relying on God, and showing courage in the face of adversity, we can then stand strong. Our adversaries see our strength and want none of it. Yet in all this arises yet another paradox; our motivation for standing strong. That motivation is love; the kind of love that does what is best for the other person.

Christian love does not retaliate in anger and malice, but, while showing strength, finds another way to resolve conflict. As one inmate who was about to be attacked said, "You don't want to try to take me down. There is 15 years of anger still under control in my body, and you do not want to unleash it." His attackers left him alone. He resolved the issue and left open a chance for ministry.

Jesus said, "I will never leave you nor forsake you." So let your strong defense, rooted in love, be your best offense.

Letter Twenty-three:
Half Full, Half Empty or a Drop

Genesis 39:20b-21a

"But while Joseph was there in prison, the Lord was with him, He showed him kindness."

Ken,

People say that a pessimist sees a glass of water as half empty while an optimist sees the glass as half full. What about the optimistic inmate whose glass holds just a drop of water?

Ken you asked me to share with you a typical day in prison. A day in prison is merely a sip of the water of life. It is easy to describe a day's routine; difficult to relate to you battles that go on in a man's mind during that routine day.

There are two enemies that threaten me constantly: Cynicism and Boredom.

The days run together. Month after month, year after year, the lights come on at 5:00 am. Simultaneously the intercom blares: "Five O'clock wake up."

It doesn't take long to get ready. I have a choice of wearing blue jeans & denim shirt with your name & number marked above the pocket pulled out from under my one-inch thick mattress. I have my devotions with the Portals of Prayer booklet and then attempt to stretch out my half-century-old joints and muscles.

At 5:30 am, the intercom interrupts the morning clatter of a mass of men getting ready, "Special Diets to Breakfast." The doors screech open echoing throughout the mega structure of concrete and steel. I'm on a cardiovascular diet, so I go.

Rushed through the line, I am handed an institutional meal. What can I say about it? The meal sustains life, yet with no satisfaction. When 800 to 1000 men must eat in a narrow, scheduled time period, then you can count on an officer coming by your table telling you to quickly move on.

As a sea blue ocean of humanity in denim shirts and blue jeans, we return to our cells to await work call. At 6:45 a.m. the doors clang open again as the intercom announces work call. To save taxpayers' money, the prison administration seeks to run as self sufficiently as possible. The inmate job assignments reflect a self-contained unit. For years I received $1.05 a day.

Lunch comes in Styrofoam trays to your worksite. A disheartening array of unrecognizable casseroles and canned vegetables along with some Jell-O is the normal cuisine. Work ends at 2:30 p.m.

We return to our rooms to be locked down again. At 3:00 p.m. there is a stand up count to make sure everyone is still around. This count happens again at 8:30 p.m. and 10:00 p.m.

Dinner is announced between 4:00 and 4:30 p.m. Later in the evening, a man has a choice between staying in his cell or going to "the yard" for recreation or going to an activity call out. These activities include various group meetings such as Lifer's Club, African Awareness group, Alcoholics Anonymous, Narcotics Anonymous, Veteran's group, etc. Your other choice can be chapel call out. In order to go to these activities you must send a form requesting to be put on the call out list two weeks in advance of the planned activities. Otherwise, you are not allowed to go.

Most evenings we are blessed with some protestant volunteers in prison ministry who for an hour and a half bring the love of Christ in their words and actions.

The day's routine ends with lights out at 10:00 p.m. Of course, every hour a correctional officer comes by to shine a flashlight into your face to make sure you are still there throughout the evening.

Each day is filled with noise and negativism. In most every aspect of this life there is always noise resonating throughout the walls. There is always the negative thought processing, the talk of disillusioned loafers infiltrating your mind. There is the constant complaining and bickering about how terrible our existence is.

Ken, this is the drop of the water of life for a man in prison. If an optimist sees the glass as half full; what should I see when there is just a little drop at the bottom of my glass?

I am thankful to our gracious Lord. For a sip of water is a precious gift to a thirsty man. The Lord provides as he always provided for Joseph. Even a drop of water is an abundant life for a sinner saved by grace.

Tom

◆ ◆ ◆

Tom,

When you wrote about the optimist who sees a half glass of water as half full instead of half empty, I thought of a comic scene in a Laurel and Hardy movie I watched as a child during the 1950s.

The rotund Ollie convinced Stan that he should share a glass of water with him. Ollie tells Stan to, "drink your half first." Looking somewhat bewildered as to how he was going to do this, Stan began drinking. Slowly, he drinks half the glass of water. At this point, Ollie expects him to hand over the glass, but he doesn't. Instead, he confidently drinks the rest of the water.

I can still picture the frustrating look on Ollie's face. He elbowed Stan in the chest and demanded to know why he drank it all. Now crying, Stan said, "My half was on the bottom."

Humor, of course, is a poor weapon against our natural inclination toward cynicism and boredom, but it can lesson its weight. And humor is a sure sign of a struggling but healthy person. So is being actively engaged in whatever opportunities present themselves.

Now I don't know how many jokes Joseph told or were told while in prison but I am sure Satan attacked him with cynicism and boredom. Still, by the power and presence of God, Joseph ultimately triumphed.

But what does the "presence of God" mean? In Gen 39:21 Moses wrote, "And God was with Joseph..."
The "presence of God" that Joseph enjoyed was the comfort of being conscious of God's presence and His favor in his life. The Holy Spirit dwelt in Joseph's heart, guiding his soul and mind; a Spirit that cannot be contained by prison walls. And so Joseph, who was tried severely in his faith, facing many dull and dangerous days that seemed without end, was not utterly downcast in spirit.

The first sign of God's divine presence was that He "made him [Joseph] the object of good will." That is, God "turned to him goodwill." And the goodwill He turned to Joseph was to care for others. In particular, "He gave him favor in the sight of the overseer." God caused the overseer to look with favor toward Joseph.
Tom, like Joseph, the Lord has given you many signs to show that He turned to you good will and He gave you favor in the sight of others. How else can the good things you have been involved in at Lansing be explained?

Yes, I have seen and heard witness that our Lord has given you signs of favor in the sight of the warden, guards and inmates — and others on the outside. Because they looked kindly upon you, you have been able to advise and write articles for the organization, I Was In Prison Ministries; to organize the first prison Marriage Enrichment Seminar for inmates and spouses; to help write bylaws for Convicts for Christ" to place Bibles in Lansing and to teach the Bible to inmates; to participate in a world record breaking single tennis marathon (five days and five hours) in 1988, where you raised more than $1600 for the Ronald McDonald House; to get your devotional booklet, *Prisoner's Reflections*, published by The Lutheran Church Missouri Synod; to serve as producer and on-camera spokesman of videos to help youth make the right choices in life — just think, more than 5000 copies of these have been sold.

You have great favor with your wife, Terry, and your three children; your extended family and hundreds of people who pray for you and are blessed by you.

These are some of the signs of good will God has showered upon you. But the basis for all this comes from your faith in Christ that cried out: "I am thankful to our gracious Lord. For a sip of water is a precious gift to a thirsty man. The Lord provides as he always provided for Joseph. Even a drop of water is an abundant life for a sinner saved by grace."

With those enduring words of faith triumphing over temporal cynicism and boredom, I was drawn to the Gospel of John (4:13,14) where Jesus said, "Whoever drinks of this water will thirst again, but whoever drinks of the water that I shall give him will never thirst. But the water that I shall give him will become in him a fountain of water springing up into everlasting life."

Tom, God knew what kind of water you were talking about and the person who gives it. The "water" is eternal life and the person who gives it is Jesus. As the water is life, so the drinking is faith; and this one act of spiritual drinking removes the human thirst forever.

Jesus assures us that the moment we obtain this "water," it becomes our possession. He brings the dead to life day after day. Once made alive, we live on. Once born anew, we need not be born again. Jesus and Jesus alone gives us this wonderful water.
Although Stan Laurel confidently drank the whole glass of water, still, a "sip" and a "drink" is all that we need for eternal life.

Blessings in Christ,

Ken

◆ ◆ ◆

A cup of water and river of life

"And He showed me a pure river of water of life, clear as crystal, proceeding from the throne of God and of the Lamb."

(Revelation 22:1)

Jesus explained to His followers that they should offer a cup of cold water to thirsty people, and do so in His name as an act of love. To the Christian who does this, Jesus counts it as if He had done it Himself.

Even a drop of the *spiritual* water that Jesus offers to all who, by faith, believe on Him quenches a person's greatest thirsts — for God, for Truth and for eternal freedom. By His death and resurrection, Jesus has given this spiritual water to you. Now that you have faith in your heart, come to Him in prayer and to His Word, and receive refreshment.

You may be at a place in life that seems like a dessert, where your spirit is parched and you want to give up. Jesus says, "Come to Me all of you who are heavy laden and I will give you rest." (Matthew 11:28) He not only will carry your burdens, but He will give you spiritual refreshment that will last through eternity. Pray, "Jesus, I believe, but help me in my unbelief. I thank you for giving me the water that you have promised." Then drink your fill of His living water as you examine His Word and obey His commands.

Then, at the end of life, the Lamb of God — Jesus, Himself — will flood over you His "pure river of water of life" as He calls you into Heaven.

He will replace your thirst for worldly refreshment with the water of life, so that you will never thirst again.

Letter Twenty-four:
No Crying In Prison

Genesis 43:30-31

"Deeply moved at the sight of his brothers, Joseph hurried out and looked for a place to weep. He went into his private room and wept there."

Ken,

A few years ago there was a movie about Women's Professional Baseball during the war years called, "A League of Their Own." In one scene, the coach was yelling at the right fielder about her failure to throw to the cut off person on the relay to home plate. The flustered female right fielder began weeping uncontrollably. The veteran coach expressed his frustration, "This is baseball! There's no crying in Baseball!" To this old timer, it was an unwritten rule that on the field of play in the great sport of baseball there is no shedding of tears.

You might say that the same unwritten code of conduct is etched on the entrance gate of every existing prison — "THERE IS NO CRYING IN PRISON!"

I look at Joseph. The Scripture records at least five times that Joseph cried. [Genesis 42:24; 43:30; 45:1-2; 14-15; 46:29] Surprisingly, it was not when Joseph was sold into slavery nor was it when he was sent to prison. It seemed for years that Joseph kept his sensitive feelings bottled up in regard to his betrayal and injustices placed upon him.

I don't know whether Egypt had an unwritten code forbidding tears while incarcerated. People of the ancient middle east were more open to expressions of feelings, more so than might be comfortable for us westerners.

A person simply cannot afford to show an expression which may portray vulnerability. Tears are interpreted as weakness. Yet Joseph remained a sensitive, caring person throughout his imprisonment and beyond.

The wise "Preacher" says in Ecclesiastes 3:1, 4, "There is a time for everything ...a time to weep and a time to laugh." I believe that even the strongest and toughest man in prison weeps sometimes. There are deaths, disappointments, separations, injustices, guilt, bad news from home; tragic stories of lives in here.

I break that unwritten "no crying" code.

I feel like crying often. But I weep rarely. The problem is that there is no privacy. Crying is a very personal, intimate action. Joseph looked for a place to weep. He went to his private room to cry. A man in prison will hold back his tears for months because places of solitude are rare. My tears flow with the stream of water from the shower nozzle at times. I weep quietly into my pillow deep in the night.

What is a man to do, Ken? I believe Joseph, because of his faith, was one of the mentally toughest men that ever lived. But his love for his Lord, his family, and his care for all mankind, made him extremely sensitive as well as tough. We are told that Joseph "kissed all his brothers and wept over them." (Gen. 45:15).

Prison can desensitize a man. Hearing some of the stories of men here in prison, I could get hardened. The less one cares, the less one hurts, and then the less one weeps.

I do not ever want to become so desensitized to the pains of the world and so institutionalized while in prison that I cannot care enough to cry.

Part of the ministry is to weep with those who weep.

Tom

◆ ◆ ◆

Tom,

Remember that day when we were students at Concordia Theological Seminary in Springfield, Illinois and a professor asked the question, "What is the shortest sentence in the Bible?" No one knew the answer so he told us, "Jesus wept." (John 11:35)
But now as I look back over those decades and consider that short sentence, I realize that it was more than a simple trivia question; more than a complex theological quiz; and without doubt, more than the simple act of crying.

You explained how tough it is to cry in prison because of the fear of showing weakness to other inmates. Yet you, like Joseph, still remain passionate and tender toward God, and toward circumstances beyond your control. So you have worked to find places of privacy in which to cry — in the shower during the day, in the bed at night. Not to do so would leave you, as it does so many other prisoners, hard-hearted.

But genuine faith in Christ produces genuine tears, that is, manly tears. They show the believer to be sensitive, loving and yet tough all at the same time.

Before I enrolled at the Seminary in 1972, my best friend was killed in Vietnam. His name was Michael Jenson. We grew up together in Fergus Falls, Minnesota. We took many classes together in high school and shared a room at Moorhead State College.

From 1967 to 1970 I served in the US Army. I knew that Michael had also joined the service and had been sent to Vietnam. Then in March 1970, I got an "early out" and went to St. Cloud State University. During May of that same year, I heard the news that Michael had been killed. His bullet-riddled and mutilated body laid there in the steamy hot jungle near the Cambodian border for two weeks before a recovery team removed it. The closed casket at his funeral made his death all the more difficult. How could I even say "good-bye" to my best friend?

Michael's father asked me to be a pallbearer. At that time, student protesters were on campus and a huge demonstration that lasted several days. As I walked to my car one day after class, I heard someone playing the Beatles song, "Here Comes The Sun." At that moment, I broke down and sobbed, weeping bitterly over the loss of a good friend Michael. I wept from the depths of my soul.

You know how I love putting on an air of being "a man," strong and athletic, unmoving. But inside, Christ has made me tender. I mourned the loss of my friend that day. I felt alone and even abandoned.

But on the day of those Vietnam protests, as I walked along the sidewalk, I pushed aside one of the protesters, wanting to provoke a fight. I knew it was wrong but I didn't care.

It took me many years to admit that what I did that day was wrong. But I thank God that He protected me. In Christ, I realized the need to repent. And through those tears, I learned to empty myself and turn to Christ for strength.

But why did I weep? Was it a weakness, or was it something more? I believe I cried for several reasons. I cried because I loved and missed Michael. I cried because I felt sorry for myself. I cried because it cleansed my spirit. Weeping brought out a rush of emotions, some good, some not so good, and some downright evil. I felt them all.

So I saw that "Jesus wept," and it meant more to me. I wanted to know more about it. In this verse, I saw with gripping brevity and without comment that Jesus wept because he loved and had genuine compassion for His friend, Lazarus, and for those who loved him. I can picture the silent tears falling from Jesus' eyes as He walked toward the tomb just before raising Lazarus from the dead. Jesus didn't fight off his emotions. He was always in perfect control of himself. Yet He wept, openly.

In other places, we know that Jesus wept in passionate sorrow over the sins of Jerusalem. And in the darkness of Gethsemane He wept so profoundly that His body gave off sweat drops of blood as He agonized over the sins of the whole world (Heb. 5:7). His were noble and manly tears.

Yes, the true God and true Man wept for you and me that day

in the Garden of Gethsemane. Our sins hurt Him and He cried for us. He cried and He died on Calvary's cross to make us acceptable to God the Father. And He is pleased when we weep over our sins.

At the bottom of this, we learn that weak men refuse to cry. We can weep and still remain strong. But one day, Tom, we shall all be with Him in heaven and then there shall be no more tears, for they shall all be wiped away. Generations of believers, all who had been prisoners of sin in this life, will be freed from their earthly prisons to sing praise to the Lamb who wept for them.

Blessings in Christ,

Ken

◆ ◆ ◆

What makes you cry?

" 'This day is holy to the Lord your God, do not mourn nor weep.' For all the people wept, when they heard the words of the Law." (Nehemiah 8:9)

People cry for many reasons.

Nehemiah had just engineered the successful rebuilding of Jerusalem's walls. He gathered all the Israelites together so that the prophet Ezra could read to them from God's Law. Upon hearing those words, the people wept bitterly. Why?

The Israelites were confronted with their own sin nature. The reading of the Law told them just how sinful they had become. Their tears resulted from a troubled conscience. But Nehemiah did not leave them in this state of sorrow; he told them to go away, eat and drink and enjoy life. "The joy of the Lord is your strength," he told them.

The Gospel of Jesus Christ liberates the sinner and replaces sinful sorrow with grateful joy. Rejoice in that you have been set free from the penalty of sin, and pardoned for eternity.

Yet, do cry. Cry at the loss of freedom, the loss of family and friends, the wayward child, your constant struggle with sin. Cry as you see others' lives destroyed by their own recklessness and rebellion. Your passion and love for others that drives you to tears is a reflection of stalwart strength — strength that comes from Jesus Christ.

Cry for joy at the good fortune of others, at your own good fortune, when a person confesses Jesus as his or her Savior.

Did you cry today? Do you walk, by faith, in Jesus Christ? If so, let Him change your tears of sorrow into tears of joy.

"Now to Him who is able to keep you from stumbling, and to present you faultless before the presence of His glory with exceeding joy, to God our Savior, who alone is wise, be glory and majesty, dominion and power, both now and forever. Amen." (Jude 1:24-25)

Letter Twenty-Five:
Guilt Rides the Guilt Ridden

Genesis 42:21

"[The brothers] said to one another, 'Surely we are being punished because of our brother. We saw how distressed he was when he pleaded with us for his life, but we would not listen; that's why this distress has come upon us.'"

Ken,

It was a long ride back from Egypt to Canaan for Joseph's brothers. The journey was long not because they rode donkeys but because Guilt rode the brothers.

Ken; let's talk about a guilt trip. We all take guilt trips sometimes. Instead of repentance before God we harbor guilt. Instead of accepting the free gift of forgiveness from the Lord, we put the saddle on and let guilt ride us.

When the brothers who had sold Joseph into slavery at least 20 years earlier came to Egypt to obtain relief from the famine, they had hoped to buy grain and leave quietly. But Joseph, unrecognized by his brothers, presented them with a dilemma. Joseph said that to prove they were not spies he was going to keep one brother in prison until the youngest, Benjamin was presented before him.

The brother's reaction was interesting. This troubling situation brought their 20-year-old guilt to the forefront. "Surely we are being punished because of our brother, [Joseph]." The image of the youngster desperately pleading for his life had been in their minds for years.

First they had wanted to kill young Joseph, and then they put him in the cistern. Eventually they settled on selling him as a slave. They turned a deaf ear to Joseph's pleadings as he went to Egypt in chains. The brother's guilt plus their present circumstances led them to conclude to each other, "That's why this distress has come upon us."

As if it was not enough to bring up guilt from years past, the brothers proceed to blame each other for sins and distress. Rueben replied, "Didn't I tell you not to sin against this boy? But you wouldn't listen! Now we must give an accounting for his blood." (Genesis 42:22). Bringing up guilt and blaming does nothing to solve their present crisis. What a pitiful plight they carry on!

All of us are tempted to be a harbinger of guilt. All of us, Ken, are tempted to bring up that guilt and let it ride on us, anytime something goes wrong in our lives. I do it. There are plenty of incidents in prison where life can go wrong. I could easily say that each turn of events for the worse goes bad because of some certain past sin. Such a life of letting guilt ride a person would bring on certain despair.

For a Christian who has repented and has received the full forgiveness in Christ, bringing up past sins as a blame for present bad happenings actually results in cheapening the precious blood of Jesus Christ. Worse yet, for a Christian to succumb to the temptation to blame others such as "the system" or "the administration" gives a false sense of relief from personal guilt. Why do the guilt ridden let guilt ride our backs?

What a terrible 20 years it must have been for these brothers to let guilt taunt them at every wrong turn. If only we could turn to the Lord Jesus Christ for full forgiveness. Then the burden would be light.

Forgiven,

Tom

❖ ❖ ❖

Tom,

This may sound harsh but I think it's true. Joseph's 10 brothers had good reason to feel the wrath of God as they prophetically testified of themselves: "Surely we are being punished because of our brother, [Joseph]." The guilt they continued to carry resulted in 20 years of needless distress. Without a doubt, the brothers most certainly knew that their trouble came as a direct result of their sin against Joseph. For God had intentionally brought them to Egypt for this meeting with Joseph, and gave them a chance to receive forgiveness.

However, I am not suggesting that every time something bad happens, it can be directly traced to the sin of the person involved; that is not true. Jesus makes this clear when His disciples asked about a blind man who pleaded with Jesus to restore his sight. The disciples wondered who had sinned that this man should be born blind from birth. Jesus said, "It was neither this man sinned, nor his parents." (John 9:2-3)

So, we have to be careful about consigning God's wrath upon people. When blame is assigned directly upon persons or nations in Scripture, it is God who assigns it, as He did to Joseph's brothers. There are, nevertheless, many difficulties in life that *are* a direct result of our sin.

With few exceptions, the diseases of AIDS and syphilis are a direct result of a sinful life-style — and in those tragic cases, such as blood transfusions or a baby born to a drug-addled mother; certainly the sin of the parent or blood donor directly contributed to the disease.

Many people declare bankruptcy and often, bankruptcy results simply from sinful acts of grossly over-spending. Such sin has a profound effect on the debtor and on the borrower and on society.

And, although it is certainly not always the case, divorce often results from the sin of the husband or the wife, or both, to live up to their responsibility in their marriage. I have had to face the effects of unconfessed sin in my life, too.

In 1987 I told you about the problem I was having with the local church and the Synod. It centered around two issues: church doctrine and administration. I sought to uphold the doctrine of our church and its constitution, and some did not like it. But that was not the only problem I faced.

Some did not agree with our synod's teachings on moral and cultural issues, and wanted to fire me. As you know, it ended up in a legal fight within the church. I survived two very bitter church trials. But the battle left a bitter taste. I made enemies — members and fellow pastors, the circuit counselor and especially the district president. I believed I was right on the issues; that I knew and still contend. But, I was so wrong in my heart, my motives and methods, for trying to uphold them. And even after surviving, I harbored ill will in my heart for those who opposed me. This was my great burden. And because I would not recognize it as sin, it made me bitter and angry over the years.

Every Sunday as I preached about repentance and forgiveness in the name of Jesus, the thought of my own lack of repentance lingered in my mind and burdened my heart. This served to make my burden even heavier, just as it did Joseph's brothers. I couldn't shake it, though I tried. Finally, there came a time when I could no longer stand the guilt that distressed my faith.

Our loving Lord kept prodding me through Word and Sacrament to do the only right thing.

So, I called on the Reverend Doctor Lane Seitz, the District President of the Minnesota South District of the LC-MS. During our meeting, I confessed my sins. I apologized to him for the self-righteous and arrogant way I went about trying to uphold Biblical truth and correcting administrative wrong. The pain I had caused him and others did not have to happen, but it did because of me.

What a relief it was for me to receive forgiveness from Pastor Seitz. A monstrous 17-year burden fell from my back and to where it belonged — on the back of Jesus Christ and on the Cross of Calvary.

Tom, like so many Christians, we say that even though God forgives us, we think that we must also go on suffering the consequences for our sin. It is true that the convict serving time for felony crime still must suffer incarceration, but his soul is set free from the bars of sin by Jesus' blood — no prison can restrain Jesus love. Yet, even these chastening experiences of life can help us mature spiritually and then give us opportunity to rejoice in God's grace all the more.

Yes, God wants all people everywhere who are heavy-laden by guilt to come to Him and find refreshment and salvation (Matt. 11:28). What a joy to know that God turns His face toward us because of Christ's great sacrifice on the Cross and now declares all believers in Christ to be a "chosen generation, a royal priesthood, an holy nation." He "has called us out of darkness into His marvelous light." (1 Peter 2:9) That makes our burden light.

Blessings in Christ,

Ken

♦ ♦ ♦

What's that on your back?

"Come to Me, all you who labor and are heavy laden, and I will give you rest. Take my yoke upon you and learn from Me, for I am gentle and lowly in heart, and you will find rest for your souls. For My yoke is easy and My burden is light." (Matthew 11:28-30)

Guilt can literally cause a person to walk humped over, as though he or she suffered some sort of curvature of the spine. Ironically, guilt can also cause some people to walk straight upright in pride and arrogance, denying the effect of their actions; believing that they are above the law and beyond guilt.

Every human being has to find a way to deal with guilt, and outside of forgiveness and pardon, there is no human way to defeat it.

If guilt is denied or ignored it creates pent-up anger and frustration that can explode into destructive, even violent and deadly behavior. Such action only adds guilt upon guilt, until the person repents, or his or her conscience becomes "seared with a hot iron..." (I Timothy 4:2)

If guilt is recognized, but he or she does not find relief, it can lead to depression, darkness and defeat — even death.

So what is that on your back? Do you carry an empty conscience as the result of ignoring and denying guilt? Or do you carry a full sack, weighed down with bricks of guilt that threaten fully to break your spirit?

Jesus calls you to Himself. He says to cast all your cares on Him, because He loves and cares for you. Will you confess your guilt to Him today? In silent prayer, just between you and Him, tell Him what you have done. Here's why:

"If we confess our sins, He is faithful and just to forgive us our sins and to cleanse us from all unrighteousness." (I John 1:9)
Having made such a confession, you can now carry on your back the cross of Jesus Christ, the One who has lifted your burden of guilt and replaced it with His salvation. Praise be to God!

Letter Twenty-Six:
Prison of Pity

Genesis 42:36

"Their father Jacob said to them, 'You have deprived me of my children. Joseph is no more, and Simeon is no more, and now you want to take Benjamin. Everything is against me!'"

Ken,

I have to laugh as I think of Jacob. Jacob would fit right in with the attitude of a large percentage of men incarcerated in our modern-day prisons. Simply put, most are full of self-pity.

I don't want to minimize the tragedies in Jacob's life. He had lost his beloved wife, Rachel, and he had lost Joseph. But where is his godly perspective? Jacob was a Patriarch. He was the bearer of the Lord's covenant promises passed through Abraham and Isaac. Jacob was blessed with 12 sons which he had by two wives and two concubines. He had been blessed with great wealth and honor for a man of his time. Yet he says to nine of his sons, "You have deprived me of my children."

Rachel had been dead for maybe 25 years and Joseph had been dead (at least in Jacob's mind) for over 20 years. It was long overdue for Jacob to adjust to these losses.

Then Jacob says, "Simeon is no more." Although Simeon was held captive in Egypt, he was alive and well and awaiting rescue when Benjamin would come down with his brothers. But Jacob already counted Simeon as gone.

Pity makes a man exaggerate his losses. And to top it all off, Jacob was terribly afraid of losing his favorite, youngest son,

Benjamin. Reuben tried to give Jacob assurance of Benjamin's safe passage by taking full responsibility as the oldest son. But Jacob would not accept Reuben's word of honor. Jacob would not be consoled and he cries out, "Everything is against me!" Reuben even said, "You may put both of my sons to death if I do not bring him back to you" (v. 37).

But incredibly Jacob's negative response was, "His brother is dead and he is the only one left" (v. 38). Oh, how that must have hurt the other nine sons of Jacob.

In prison it can seem like everything is against us — the public, the administration, the correctional officers, the parole board, other inmates and even family members. Every step of the way there seems to be opposition against an incarcerated man trying to build back his life or make any progress in becoming a useful member of society again. Self-pity can grip a man, preventing him from taking steps toward freedom.

While on the prison yard three days before Christmas, I walked by a young man that I had seen often in the visiting room with his wife and two young sons. I asked Tony how he was doing. He said, "Terrible!" Then he asked if he could walk with me and talk. It was 20 degrees with a brisk Kansas prairie wind chill. Amidst the tears and the frozen snot on his mustache, he explained as we walked that his wife had told him that she wanted a divorce, she had found another man, and that she was taking the children out of state. He said there was no use living anymore. I knew that nine of ten marriages with an incarcerated spouse end in divorce.

Stats do not help a devastated man. I shared that life does not depend on another person's decision but on the Lord's promises. Tony will make it another day holding on to faith, instead of self-pity.

Pity can hold a man captive much more effectively than any prison walls. There have been days that I have cried out to God, "Everything is against me!" But I am reminded immediately of Romans 8:31, "If God is for us, who can be against us?" This type of self-pity is simply a lack of faith.

So self-pity be gone!

"He who did not spare his own Son, but gave Him up for us all — how will He not also, along with Him, graciously give us all things?" (Romans 8:32) Pity paralyzes a person, keeping him from taking risks. We cannot out of the same mouth continue to say, "Everything is against me," and "God has blessed me." In contrast to Jacob, Joseph, who had every reason to feel self-pity, maintained the attitude that though circumstances were bad, God was always with him.

Blessings in Christ,

Tom

◆ ◆ ◆

Tom,

"Then it happened as they emptied their sacks, that surprisingly each man's bundle of money was in his sack; and when they and their father saw the bundles of money, they were afraid. And Jacob their father said to them, 'You have bereaved me: Joseph is no more, Simeon is no more, and you want to take Benjamin. Everything is against me.' Then Reuben spoke to his father, saying, 'Kill my two sons if I do not bring him back to you; put him in my hands, and I will bring him back to you. But he said, 'My son shall not go down with you, for his brother is dead, and he is left alone. If any calamity should befall him along the way in which you go, then you would bring down my gray hair with sorrow to the grave.' " (Genesis 42:35-38)

You're right when you say, "Pity makes a man exaggerate his losses." It's apparent from the text that Jacob and his sons forgot God's covenant promise and for a moment sat mired in self-pity. But Jacob's self-pity differed from his sons', and as you point out, made no sense in a larger view of his life.

When Joseph's brothers uncovered "bundles of money" in their sacks, immediately they felt convicted even though they had done nothing wrong. That their conscience bothered them is indicated where the text says, "they were afraid." They must have said to themselves, "How are we going to explain this?" For such a discovery required an explanation, one they couldn't give, and the fact that they had the money made them vulnerable to serious criminal charges. Even Jacob might accuse them of stealing the money from Pharaoh. And he might charge them with lying. Since they were reluctant to come clean about Joseph's death 20 years earlier when their sinful human nature forced them into a cover-up.

But look at what Jacob said to them. His courage fell far short of rock solid faith when he suggested that all of his sons were in danger. That he exaggerated in this situation seems clear from the fact that 10 of his sons stood right in front of him — only one stayed behind in Egypt.

Why did Jacob overstate the case? I agree with you that it was self-pity and a lack of faith. For self-pity, in the end, can always be traced back to a shallow faith. I know that personally.
And, personally, I find a lot of comfort in Jacob's self-pity because if the righteous patriarch demonstrated such a lack of faith in times of sorrow, especially in light of God's covenant promise to him, how much more consolation will God shower upon a sinner like me? If Jacob and his sons can be forgiven for their lapse into fear, doubt and self-pity then I, too, have the same hope.

I suppose from his sons' point of view, Jacob hit closer to the truth than he knew as he charged his sons of being responsible for making him childless. Now, those nine sons standing there (excluding Benjamin) must have cringed at his words. They must have wondered if he really knew the truth, and were afraid to ask! Since they had never repented of this evil, they cover up the truth.
Tom, I'm convinced that self-pity is one of those inevitable states of mind into which we all fall from time to time. Still, self-pity is sinful even though it is something we humans remain unable to prevent or to correct on our own. Only the Gospel can correct it. It makes a gift to us of God's grace, remission of sins, eternal righteousness and life, and delivers us from all terrors and condemnation of the law. The Gospel hands us the consolation that all our debt had been paid by the Son of God, Jesus Christ Himself.

I may not sit in a physical prison experiencing self-pity over how others allegedly treat me. But just as everyone else, I have experienced self-pity, more than I would like to admit.

In May 1980, I was asked by the president of the American Legion Club in Waldorf, Minnesota, to give a Memorial Day speech at the local high school. I spoke about the many sacrifices made by true heroes of the Revolutionary and Civil Wars. They gave their lives for freedom. After naming some of the lesser-known heroes of those wars, I talked about my friend, Michael Jenson, who died in Vietnam (1970). As I told the story, I mentioned that Michael's father (Henry) had asked me to be a pallbearer at his son's funeral. The memory and sorrow overwhelmed me and I broke down and cried.

My public tears embarrassed me, made me feel foolish. And I felt sorry for myself.

Later that day I talked to some Waldorf people about my embarrassment. Almost to a person they said, "Pastor, don't worry about it. When you cried, it told us you cared...that you're human. And that's good."

They made me feel good. Very good, in fact! But, there was a downside to it.

I turned their sympathy for my emotional state into self-pity instead of sorrow for Michael's death. Sad, isn't it?! I started out honoring a friend and war hero and ended up feeling sorry for myself. How pathetic is that!

And like the sons of Jacob, pride got the better of me. But as Joseph eventually forgave his brothers of their evil, I, too received Christ's forgiveness.

Perhaps that's why I love this story of Jacob so much because it reminds me of God's wonderful mercy and grace in Christ Jesus who sacrificed His life on the cross for weak and sinful people, like Jacob, his sons and me.

Blessings in Christ,

Ken

◆ ◆ ◆

Wet diapers and cold mud

"He also brought me up out of a horrible pit, out of the miry clay, and set my feet upon a rock, and established my steps." (Psalm 40:2)

A friend once said, "Self-pity is a little like sitting in a wet diaper. At first it feels warm and soothing, but soon, it begins to stink and irritate." So it is.

We all fall into the miry clay of self-pity from time to time. As we realize it, in our fight to escape, in an ironic way, we actually enjoy the battle. We tell others, "It's not my fault. I didn't make this happen." And in that, we might even be right. But instead of freeing us from the pit, we fall deeper into the pit until it just feels like cold mud, trapping and about to overwhelm us.

We blame others. We blame circumstances. We blame judges, juries, snitches, sisters, brothers, pastors, teachers, politicians — the list is endless. The list is meaningless.

It can be different.

A wet diaper can be exchanged for a dry, clean one, fresh with the scent of detergents that have scrubbed it clean. We can be lifted out of the miry clay by the hands of the One who loves us most, and washed clean and made whole.

Will you take the first step of faith away from self-pity? Thank God in faith that Jesus has paid for your sins, and ask Him to lift you up and free you from the clutches of self-pity. He will set your feet on a solid rock. Then you will receive peace and bring blessings to others. For God, who lifts you up, is the same One who "...has put a new song in [your] mouth — praise to our God; many will see it and fear, and will trust in the Lord." (Psalm 40:3)

Letter Twenty-Seven:
Forgiving Living

Genesis 50:15-21

"When Joseph's brothers saw that their father was dead, they said, 'What if Joseph holds a grudge against us and pays us back for all the wrongs we did to him?'...But Joseph said to them, 'Don't be afraid. Am I in the place of God? You intended to harm me, but God intended it for good to accomplish what is now being done, the saving of many lives...'"

Ken,

All that we have written in the past in regard to Joseph — all the topics, the lessons — they are nothing unless we confront the concept of forgiveness. I consider this subject as the foremost personal issue in the story of Joseph and one of the most important issues in my life.

For the 10 brothers of Joseph the situation came to a head after Jacob, their father, died. These brothers had not really changed in the many years since plotting to kill and then opting to sell Joseph into slavery. Fear, jealousy, hatred and selfishness still ruled their hearts.

I hope I am not being too harsh. But, Ken, their fearful behavior did not come from observations of Joseph's Godly character. They were not thinking about whom Joseph really was or God's work in all these years. They were thinking, "If I were Joseph, with his power, I would imprison, torture, or kill us for what we have done to him."

They actually went on to think, "Dad is dead. Nothing will prevent Joseph from getting revenge against us." Even in asking for forgiveness, they lied without even the courage to come face to face with Joseph. They sent an emissary who implored their father's name and God's name in a lie: "Now please forgive the sins of the servants of the God of your father." (v. 17) It was a desperate lie.

The brothers lied. Joseph wept.

Many speculate as to why Joseph wept here. I believe Joseph wept because he was terribly saddened by the fact that his 10 brothers had for so long completely missed the whole point of a Godly life. They were imprisoned by guilt and fear. Joseph saw that these men, ruled by guilt, could try to manipulate him by sending an emissary to lay guilt on Joseph with a lie and then maybe get forgiveness. Joseph wept at their sad, sad state of mind.

Ironically, in fulfillment of Joseph's dream that started this saga, the brothers threw themselves down and said, "We are your slaves." (v. 18) All they could see was Joseph's power and their own frailness. All Joseph could see was God's power and his own humble frailness.

"Am I in the place of God?" Joseph asked (v. 19). They feared. Joseph forgave.

Living by grace, Joseph was predisposed to forgive even before the brothers asked for forgiveness. There were no conditions to be met before he forgave. There were no prerequisites on the part of those in need of forgiveness. They did not have to manipulate Joseph into giving forgiveness nor did they have to persuade him by guilty feelings into forgiveness.

To forgive is foremost to a child of God. It was Joseph's nature to forgive throughout his whole ordeal knowing by faith God will fulfill His purposes. Therefore, Joseph would live to forgive.

In my daily prayers, I would choke, stutter and stammer during the Lord's Prayer at the phrase, "forgive us our trespasses as we forgive those who trespass against us," if I were not living forgiving. I carry no grudges, no bitterness, and no vengefulness in my life. I live with a predisposition to forgive.

It is risky to live to forgive. People can take advantage of you. Those who meant me harm and used me I forgave. This is not because I am special; but because God is special as revealed in His Son, Jesus Christ. We love because He first loved us. We forgive because He first forgave us. We make the best of our circumstances because God has already meant the circumstances for our good.

All Joseph's living was forgiving. In regard to his circumstances in life, with every drop, he got back up and rose to the top. Knowing God means everything for the good, "for the saving of many lives…" (v. 20)

Joseph was free to respond with forgiving kind of living. He would forgive the slave drivers, Potiphar's wife, the prison guards, the cupbearer who forgot him, as well as his brothers.

While I am imprisoned, I am still free to forgive. The forgiven lead forgiving lives. So Joseph forgave his brothers. And Joseph "reassured them and spoke kindly to them." (v. 21).

Like Joseph, I truly am committed to forgiving kind of living for Christ's sake.

In Christ,

Tom

◆ ◆ ◆

"Therefore, if anyone is in Christ, he is a new creation; old things have passed away; behold, all things have become new. Now all things are of God, who has reconciled us to Himself through Jesus Christ, and has given us the ministry of reconciliation, that is, that God was in Christ reconciling the world to Himself, not imputing their trespasses to them, and has committed to us the word of reconciliation." (II Corinthians 5:17-19)

Tom,

Why is it so hard to forgive?
Is it because forgiveness means more than just saying the

words, "I forgive you?" Does forgiveness not also mean that we must forgive freely from our heart? And as a result, won't we have to give up our anger, resentment and any ideas of revenge? True forgiveness means all of these things.

But there is more.

As you said, Tom, we love because God first loved us; and we forgive because He first forgave us. So, both true forgiveness and our own willingness to forgive come as a life-giving gift from God. When Jesus said that He came to give us an abundant life, I am sure He meant that such a life would be lived without the bitterness resulting from a lack of forgiveness.

Joseph lived that forgiveness. Appointed by Pharaoh as the second in command over all of Egypt, he had complete freedom — free to resent and punish his brothers, or free to forgive and bless them. I don't think his choice was an easy one to make.

We encourage people to say, "I'm sorry," and that is good, but we should also encourage the other party to say, "I forgive you." I have often wondered which is easier to say, "I'm sorry," or "I forgive you."

In the gospel of Matthew (9:1-8), Jesus announced to a paralyzed man the forgiveness of his sins. The Scribes angrily charged Jesus with blasphemy; they said no one can forgive sins but God. So Jesus told the paralytic to get up and walk, and he did. Now, Jesus looked those Scribes in the eye and asked which is easier: to forgive sins or to make a paralyzed man walk?

Well, the answer is neither, since both are miracles of God and only God can perform them. With those words, Jesus, the man, announced to the Scribes that He is also God.

It is the same with repentance and forgiveness. Both are miracles of faith and both are gifts of God. They are impossible for man to accomplish on his own but easy for our Lord to work them in us.

Oh, it's easy to say to my wife, "Katherine, I'm sorry I forgot to pick up the groceries. I'll get them later." Yet, in other instances, when I "know" that I am right and later find out that I am wrong, what do I do? Do I go to Katherine and say, "I'm sorry, you were right?" That is far harder to do.

But with my indifference, here is what I have done. First, I will have wronged her by insisting I was right. Then I will have wronged her again by refusing to say I am sorry. And, finally, I have wronged my Savior. So refusing to say I am sorry compounds the problem.

On the other hand, offering forgiveness is just as difficult, maybe even more so.

A few years back one of my Confirmation students was struggling in class. His mother thought I was picking on him. She became so upset with me that she lied to the elders about what I was teaching the children. She claimed that I taught that all Catholics were going to Hell. Well, her charge hurt me deeply. I have never taught that. In fact, I make a point of emphasizing the love and mercy of God in Christ for all people. I taught that all people, no matter what denomination they belong to, will go to heaven when they believe in Jesus Christ as their Lord and Savior.

Her charges hurt doubly because of the accusations I had to withstand through two church trials years earlier. I could feel the weight of her lies begin to take a toll on me, spiritually, emotionally and physically.

So upset did she become that she left our church and I could never say to her, "I forgive you." But what lingered on in my heart was the sinful resentment I had for her.

Tom, I know there are several people who harmed you and who will never put themselves in the position of hearing you forgive them. Yet, as you point out, you have done so.

So from my heart I forgave this woman, though she may never hear the words from my mouth. I thank Jesus daily for placing in my heart the desire to say I am sorry, and then also to say, "I forgive you." Although this does not happen near enough.

This is the point at which the Almighty God intervenes. "God was in Christ reconciling the world to Himself, not imputing their trespasses to them, and has committed to us the word of reconciliation."

Here is the source of all true forgiveness. Here is the reason we can forgive. And as I look at this passage and wonder upon the phrase, "not imputing their trespasses to them," I am elated. To imagine that God, in His heart, did not count my sins against me —

He forgave me — is astounding. And He did it while I was still a sinner.

So, in Christ, we are always living in forgiveness and living to forgive.

Tom, like Joseph and yourself, "I am committed to forgiving kind of living for Christ's sake." And I pray that some day Kansas will say, "I am sorry," in answer to your words, "I already forgave you."

Blessings in Christ,

Ken

◆ ◆ ◆

Total and absolute freedom

"Then Jesus said, 'Father forgive them, for they do not know what they do'..." (Luke 23:34)

Jesus had no guilt. He had committed no crime. His heart toward God and man was perfect. Yet He hung dying on a cross, beaten, bruised and bloody.

Not one of the men who had done these terrible deeds to Him repented, realized they had the wrong man, and told Him they were sorry for their deadly deeds.

Yet, He forgave them.

Jesus forgave them. Let that thought sink in for a moment.

Do this:

Imagine yourself in Jesus presence during those last hours of His life.

Stand in the High Priest's chambers as His detractors condemned Jesus with their lying testimony; He stood silent.

Stand in Pilate's courtroom as he made a political deal, freed a guilty man, and handed Jesus over to those who hated Him.

Stand at the foot of the cross and look on His body. Hear Him say, "It is finished."

Stand at His tomb, and see the Roman soldiers posted, making sure that no one stole His body. A huge stone lay against the cave.

Now, stand behind the women who went to refresh His body, but found the stone rolled away and the tomb empty!

See the disciples react in fear, guilt and then over-whelming joy as He stood among them; His eyes were filled with love and forgiveness!

Stand with those same disciples as they watched Him ascend into heaven.

Now, see yourself standing before the throne of God as He says, come child, you have been forgiven, my Son paid your penalty, your debt is paid in full. Welcome. You belong here.

This, then, is total and absolute freedom, all made possible because Jesus died on the cross to forgive your sins.

You have freedom by faith in Christ. In the same way, you can forgive others, even those who do not want your forgiveness, or who have hurt you the most. This is absolute freedom.

The law of love, excerpted from *Caged Bird*

This excerpt comes from the trail transcript of Tom Bird's 1984 trial for solicitation to commit murder. His attorney, Irving Shaw, had asked the question.

"You've used the term 'Christian love.' What does that mean to you, Pastor?"

"I believe in open relationships. I mean open emotions and feelings and sharing," Tom answered. "And Christian love means when someone hurts, you hurt with them; when someone mourns, you mourn with them; when someone is happy, you're happy with them and that you accept people where they're at; who they are. You don't judge them; you don't put conditions upon them."

<u>As of this publication:</u>
Tom Bird is still preaching the
Gospel as he serves his life sentence in Kansas.

Ken Kothe is still preaching the Gospel at Redeemer Lutheran Church in Burnsville, Minnesota.

Dave Racer is still writing books and stories, and tutoring about American government in St. Paul, Minnesota.

About the Authors

[Rev.] Thomas P. Bird, [41458]

Graduated with a Masters of Divinity — Mdiv. — from Concordia Seminary, Springfield, Illinois, in 1976 (a seminary of the Lutheran Church-Missouri Synod). Later he received his Masters of Sacred Theology — STM — from Concordia Seminary, Fort Wayne, Indiana, and had set his path toward receiving a Th.D.

Tom served as Senior Pastor at two churches in West Memphis, Arkansas. In 1982, he and his family moved to Emporia, Kansas where he became the Senior Pastor at Faith Lutheran Church. In 1984, a Lyon County jury found him guilty of Solicitation to Commit Murder in the death of Martin Anderson. In 1985, a different Lyon County jury found him guilty of First Degree Murder in the death of his wife Sandra. A 1990 Geary County Jury found him not guilty of the murder of Martin Anderson.

Tom has resided at Lansing Correctional Facility, Lansing, Kansas, since early in September, 1984. Tom founded a chapter of Convicts for Christ at L.C.F., wrote and produced two videos to help teenagers avoid a life of crime, helped found Marriage Enrichment Seminars inside L.C.F. to help strengthen the families of incarcerated men. He married his wife Terry in August, 1988, in a prison ceremony. Tom has three adult children.

Rev. Kenneth P. Kothe

Graduated from Concordia University, St. Paul, Minnesota, with a Bachelor of Arts Degree in 1972. He graduated with a Masters in Theology from Concordia Seminary, Springfield, Illinois, in 1976, as a classmate of Tom Bird's (a seminary of the Lutheran Church-Missouri Synod).

Pastor Kothe served as Senior Pastor to a church near Parkers Prairie, and in Waldorf, both in Minnesota. The Redeemer Lutheran Church of Burnsville, Minnesota, called him as Senior Pastor in 1983, a position he has filled for more than two decades.

Pastor Kothe has written and seen published numerous theological and church-related articles in "Christian News" and has worked for Tom Bird's freedom since 1984. He is the CEO and President of Free Tom Bird, Inc.

Pastor Kothe and his wife Katherine have four adult children and several grandchildren and reside in Burnsville, Minnesota.

Dave Racer

Dave has written more than 15 books, including the 736-page *Caged Bird*, that chronicles the life of Tom Bird. He has also edited other published books, written pamphlets, teaching materials and opinion columns.

Dave served as National Campaign Manager for Alan Keyes for President, 1996, and has served as a campaign consultant to numerous gubernatorial, State Senate and State House candidates, and has, himself, been a four-time endorsed candidate for the Minnesota Legislature.

Dave and his wife Rosanne live in St. Paul, Minnesota and have five children and two grandchildren. He is an active member of First Evangelical Free Church in Maplewood, Minnesota.

Dave wrote and produced 34 editions of "Dave Racer's Minnesota Report," a monthly tabloid newspaper (1987-1990); has written and produced more than 300 radio commentaries; hosted a daily and weekly talk radio show, *The Dave Racer Show*, from 1990 until 2001 on Twin Cities radio stations. He has designed, and manages, several websites.

Dave teaches American Government, Contemporary Issues, and Student Senate at Roseville, Minnesota, academy.

To contact one or all of the authors, write to:

Alethos Press LLC
PO Box 600160
St. Paul, MN 55106

Or Email To:
alethospress@comcast.net